Seventh-Inning Stretch

"*Seventh-Inning Stretch* is a Home Run with God at the plate! I found the stories entertaining, but I was really touched by the Biblical Afterthoughts. A must read by every man."

—Darryl Strawberry, Evangelist, Author and Four-Time MLB World Series champion.

"You had me at whiffle ball. Absolutely love *Seventh-Inning Stretch* as it immediately took me back to childhood. Dennis, you've shown us that we know the beginning and the end — it's the journey that makes us who we are and whose we are. Sometimes life seems so big and overwhelming but when we break it down to the little stories, lessons, and friends that we encounter along the way, we find that our Creator has given us the tools that equip us to overcome any obstacles we face. We are not alone. It's the stories and lessons that help us become who we are meant to be. Play ball!"

—Jim "The Rookie" Morris

"A delightful, often funny, and engaging book. Dennis' style makes for an easy and enjoyable read but the lessons learned are deep and pervasive. His ability to connect the many everyday experiences of our lives to the true meaning and value of life is poignant. I would highly recommend *Seventh-Inning Stretch* to all ages, even very young readers."

—Emily ("Missy") Crisp, Educator, Entrepreneur, Former Executive Committee Member USGA, MGA Distinguished Service Award recipient, MGA GOLFWORKS and The First Tee of Metropolitan of New York

"Everyone loves a good story. We like them even better when we're in them! Or can identify with the characters or incidents in those stories. Well, Dennis Labriola has written a gem! In his Seventh Inning Stretch, I found a lot of myself in many of those chapters, almost echoing the same thoughts and feelings Dennis has written about. It is a winsome reminder of when families and neighbors and simple things in life brought us a type of joy that seems to be missing today. Pick it up and smile."

—**Joe Battaglia,**
President of Renaissance Communications
Producer, broadcaster and author of
The Politically Incorrect Jesus and *Unfriended: Finding True Community in our Disconnected Culture*

"Through the day-to-day events of life shared in *Seventh-Inning Stretch* Dennis causes us to pause to see God's hand in the small and great things. I laughed, reflected, cried and learned about God's heart."

—**Pastor Ted Bichsel,** Pastor of Marriage,
Men and Care Ministries—Smithtown Gospel Tabernacle

"*Seventh-Inning Stretch* is a rare gem. A book of nostalgic stories which awakened my own memories. The Afterthoughts remind us of how God is present in all the moments of our lives. An easy but powerful read."

—**Dr. Andrew Sirlin,** CEO Sirlin Success Systems,
President Corporate Culture Solutions

"What a wonderful diversion from the demands of business and life. My good friend, Dennis, provides a much appreciated reprieve from the day-to-day and provides a moment to refocus on God's constant interaction with each of us. *Seventh-Inning Stretch*... recommended to everyone."

—**Vinny Papparlardo,** Entrepreneur

"*Seventh-Inning Stretch* is a book I couldn't put down. You will connect with many of Dennis' Stories and be blessed with the message he delivers. This book is truly an amazing experience for the soul."

—**Kevin J. Breen,** Entrepreneur, Chairman Men's Discipleship Network, Inc.

SEVENTH-INNING
STRETCH

Reflections on
the Game of Life

DENNIS LABRIOLA

NASHVILLE

NEW YORK • LONDON • MELBOURNE • VANCOUVER

Seventh-Inning Stretch

Reflections on the Game of Life

Published in New York, New York, by Morgan James Publishing. Morgan James is a trademark of Morgan James, LLC. www.MorganJamesPublishing.com

Proudly distributed by Ingram Publisher Services.

www.dennislabriola.com

Morgan James BOGO™

A **FREE** ebook edition is available for you or a friend with the purchase of this print book.

CLEARLY SIGN YOUR NAME ABOVE

Instructions to claim your free ebook edition:
1. Visit MorganJamesBOGO.com
2. Sign your name CLEARLY in the space above
3. Complete the form and submit a photo of this entire page
4. You or your friend can download the ebook to your preferred device

ISBN 9781631957260 paperback
ISBN 9781631957277 ebook
Library of Congress Control Number: 2021943506

Cover Design by:
Megan Dillon
megan@creativeninjadesigns.com

Interior Design by:
Christopher Kirk
www.GFSstudio.com

Morgan James is a proud partner of Habitat for Humanity Peninsula and Greater Williamsburg. Partners in building since 2006.

Get involved today! Visit MorganJamesPublishing.com/giving-back

TABLE OF CONTENTS

ACKNOWLEDGMENTS

I n a way, this entire book is a collection of acknowledgments to those who contributed to my life—not only those found within the stories and memories, but also all who taught and instructed me, by words and/or experiences, though not mentioned on the pages herein.

First, to my Lord and Savior, Jesus, may all glory and honor be Yours. Thank You for always being present.

To my wife, Patty, you are the manifestation of God's grace toward me. Thank you for your support, love, and especially for the inspiration to put these stories to paper. Without your encouragement, this work would not exist.

Special acknowledgment and thanks to my primary co-conspirators and partakers of most of my childhood endeavors.

To my sister, Connie Dunne, thanks for taking and diverting most of the attention by being the only female grandchild (until Laura showed up). Your moniker of "Queenie" was well earned and always endearing.

To my brother, Paul Labriola, the best brother any man could have. Proud to run with you for all these years.

To my more extended family of cousins, aunts, uncles, and grandparents, you are how "legacy" is defined.

To my granddaughters, Emily, Elizabeth, Kayla, and Jessica, you are the best part of me.

To my son-in-law, Kevin, know that you are an answer to prayer, a man I am so proud of, and someone I am blessed to have as my "son."

To my daughter, ChristyJeanne, you are my miracle gift from God. You always brought your mom and me great joy. Whether playing ball, expanding your pet kingdom, singing songs of worship, or now, as a beautiful woman and mother, you always carry the presence of the Lord. There is nothing better one can say about another human being. Love you always.

To my daughter, Stephanie, you entered my life a bit later and what a wonderful gift you have been as your mom and I have built a life together. To me, our relationship will always be extra special. Love you more than you know.

To my current "in-law" family (is there such a thing?), the Coccaro and Durso families. Thank you for accepting and loving me and for enriching my life. What blessings.

To my mom and dad, Julia and Anthony, thank you for always believing in me, providing the room to grow, and for being great examples of how to live. Mom, I miss you.

See you when I get there. Dad, you are my hero, instructing me as to how to be a man of steel and velvet.

To Scott and Debbie Caesar, dearest friends and supporters. Scott, thank you for all your insight, guidance, and for writing a wonderful foreword. I pray Father God is pleased.

To Arlyn Lawrence and the Inspira Literary Solutions staff for their patience, instruction, and inspiration.

To David Hancock and the crew at Morgan James Publishing, thanks for taking a chance on me and for the highest level of integrity.

FOREWORD

We all love stories. A good story, whether from Hollywood, church, or told by a friend, is like a warm blanket on a cold winter night. Our favorite stories, at times, are the ones about ourselves—stories of our lives that have matured and molded us into who we are today.

How many of us remember Christmas morning as a child? First, there is the story of Christ's birth and His magnificent message of love. Then, our euphoric rush of expectation and beloved family time. Do you remember your first sporting event with your dad? How about your first crush on a girl? Then, how it felt when you found out she liked you too.

You see, that's what stories do. They connect our lives and hearts. Stories imprint values upon us. We in turn hand them down to our children and their children. Stories create tradition. Tradition transcends time.

My friend Dennis Labriola's story is one of trial and prevailing success by many standards. He has excelled in the business arena and social circles of life, even greater in his spiritual and family life. Dennis is a longtime friend who has lived the "been there, done that" part of life. As a teacher, Dennis combines practical application and joy throughout his stories in this book, *Seventh-Inning Stretch*. As a men's discipleship coach, his wonderful wisdom and guidance will benefit you as it has for many men, including myself.

These stunning stories about Dennis' life will have you laughing, crying, or maybe just cracking a smile as you learn a life lesson or two from him within the pages of *Seventh Inning Stretch*. He has written some wonderful short stories, but none greater than the story of his relationship with the Author of Life, Jesus Christ. And, I pray Dennis' "Afterthought" section for each story will be a blessing to you as it was for me.

Scott Caesar
Author, *The Mission-Driven Man*
Men's Pastor and Founder
Men's Discipleship Network

INTRODUCTION

L ife moves and passes so quickly. So often, we find ourselves thinking back and discovering that the events most memorable in our lives are often unspoken and, therefore, unfortunately lost, never reaching those people who may benefit the most from hearing or reading about them.

Over the years, as inspiration moved me, I penned some memorable events that occurred in my life. One day, as I reorganized my desk, I came across a folder that contained these thoughts, inspirations, and fond recollections. I found one about the first time my Dad brought me to a Major League baseball game, and read it to my wife, Patty. She inquired if I had ever read this to my Dad. My response was that I hadn't. In fact, I hadn't even thought about it. Patty suggested that I rectify this and share it with him since it was a great expression of our relationship and love for one another. After some insistent prodding, I agreed that this was something I needed to do as he was in his mid-nineties. The outcome was wonderfully emotional for both of us, and the experience prompted me to realize the value of the memories of one's life. I then took pause to reflect more deeply on my own life, thus leading to the creation of this book, *Seventh-Inning Stretch*.

This collection of memories and little stories all have one thing in common: they involve the people in my life who have poured into me whatever they had to give—some much, some little, but all having great value to me, the recipient of their love and kindness. Most of these givers of wonderful gifts in my life may never know their magnificent influence on my life.

This collection is my attempt to express my acknowledgment and gratitude—although how do you assign value to those things that make you what and who you are? How do you show appreciation for something as definable as one's own DNA? Each input from the lives around us develops who we are, who we are to become, and who we are to touch. This is truly "a circle of life."

I believe in a great Creator, the initial molder of all life—that I am created in His image, and, though flawed in every way by the fall of the man Adam, am redeemed by the Lord Jesus Christ. Ultimately, He is the beginning and the end of each and every life. This genius, master design of the Creator for each of us necessitates, requires, and even demands that each life is to be connected to every other life as it navigates through this world and grows from infancy to its last moments. Not every touch or influence may be positive or even good, but God expects us to use each influence and take the "good" from it. We are to use it to strengthen and cause growth in our soul.

This is not an easy thing, but I hope these short stories help in some small way to illuminate this God-given ability we all have to draw the good from our lives, and will encourage you to start looking for how to do the same in yours. Perhaps, as you read and reflect, you will remember the people and circumstances God placed in your life, over the years, to teach you, encourage you, refine you, and lead you. Take note of them. If they are still alive, you may even wish to reach out to them and tell them how much their life mattered to you. It may just make their day!

1

MY FIRST GAME

I believe the year was 1960. I was seven years old and on my way to my first Major League baseball game with my dad. He had secured box seats from my uncle's company—field level, right behind home plate, about half-way up. My excitement was uncontainable!

We were driving to the Bronx from my home out on Long Island. The evening was perfect, at least as I remember it—a warm and clear summer's night. The wait on the way to the stadium was unbearable; the drive seemed to take hours! When we were approaching the Tri-Borough Bridge, Dad finally said, "It won't be long now." It was a few miles up the Major Deegan Expressway to the 161st Street exit and behold, directly in front of me was the most sacred place on Earth (to a seven-year-old from Long Island): Yankee Stadium.

My mind raced. I couldn't believe we were really there. But wait! We still had to park. My small heart was distressed as I took in the line of cars ahead of us. I cried, "Dad, can't we just pull over anywhere?"

He responded with his normal calmness, "The parking lot is just up ahead." I was convinced he was enjoying my agony. He was actually smiling.

Finally, we parked in one of those parking garages with multiple floors and ramps in between. There were cars everywhere. I couldn't wait to get inside. My thoughts and imaginations tumbled around in my head and overflowed out of my mouth. *There's the big bat structure outside the main entrance.* "Wait, Dad, there's a guy selling stuff. I need a Yankee cap and a scorecard!"

"Okay," he said.

Good, now I'm ready.

We stepped up to the turnstile, where Dad gave the attendant our tickets. He ripped them right in half. *What are you doing?* I screamed to myself. *Aren't the tickets good?* The attendant handed my dad the ticket stubs and we were allowed through. *I guess the tickets were okay, after all.*

My seven-year-old mind couldn't believe the sheer number of people spread out before us as we entered the ballpark. Dad took me by the hand and escorted me through the maze of people into the stadium and through what seemed like a tunnel that sloped upward. I was unable to see a thing for all the people towering above me. Then, suddenly, as I approached the top of the ramp, I was frozen in absolute amazement . . . There it was, before my very eyes, the inside of Yankee Stadium. *How did they get the grass so green?* I wondered incredulously. *It must be magic. A magical place.*

As we walked to our seats, I heard the voice of Bob Sheppard over the loudspeakers, "Ladies and gentlemen, welcome to Yankee Stadium!" It was like God's own voice speaking down to me from heaven.

Out on the field I could see *my* team warming up. Among them, I could make out some of baseball's greats: Yogi Berra, Roger Maris, and... "There he is!" I shouted, "Number 7—Mickey Mantle!" I couldn't believe it. I was at "The House that Ruth Built," looking down from my seat, observing all my heroes. Now, in my mind's eye, I recall the memory of my small hand disappearing into my father's. I felt his love and strength. There I am, once again, with my real hero.

He brought me to my first game, bought me my Yankee cap, and would get me a hot dog a little later. Afterwards, he would carry me to my bed from my contented sleep in the car on the way home. Wow, what a game!

Afterthought: The Value of a Father's Love

The song "Good, Good Father" comes to mind every time I think of my dad, and that causes me to think about my–our—Heavenly Father. It also brings me to a place of thanksgiving as I know that so many men lack a "good dad" in their lives.

As I reflect on this, I've come to realize that there is great value in a father's love that assists in the building of a man. Conversely, the absence of this love impedes a man's ability to fulfill his God-given destiny, thus preventing him from establishing his true identity as God designed. Our earthly fathers are just like us: flawed, imperfect, defective, broken men who lead lives wrought with strife. What should we—can we—expect from such men? The word "reproduction" means to make a copy. The broken father can only reproduce broken children–broken sons. And worse, the absent father leaves a void, a hole, an emptiness that sends the godly definition of adulthood, manhood, and maturity, into the abyss.

The truth is we have one good and perfect Father as Jesus demonstrated when He taught His disciples the Lord's Prayer—one who absolutely and unconditionally loves and accepts us just as we are, one who forgives, cleanses, and raises up. Whether we have had a good dad, a troubled dad, or no dad at all, our Heavenly Fathers knows what we need, what we lack, and the mess we may be. Only He can fulfill all we need. Only He can fix the magnitude of our brokenness. Only He can complete the created masterpiece of me–of you.

Maybe that's the point. We so often focus on the areas of ourselves that are lacking, broken, deficient, and ugly that we never see the hand of the Master at work in ourselves. Our default belief is often that, if we are without a proper role model, we cannot develop into the man we were intended to be. We look to our dads or lack thereof and decide we can be no better than the template we have been provided. THAT'S A LIE! Instead, we should embrace the truth that Father God is all the "father" we need. Look! God knows our plight, the cards we've been dealt, and the struggle for our mind and body survival. He understands why we are the way we are. And, He says, "So what?" This is not His intent for us.

God created us in His perfect image, not in the image of an imperfect or gone-astray dad. Let us not look where we came from, what we came from, or who we came from, but have hope and confidence in our Heavenly Father not to leave us in our current condition. As He presents Himself before us, He will command us to *"stand up and be the man"*—act the man and not the child. We can be more than we are if we let God do His thing with us. As the Good Book says, "…be confident of this very thing, that He who has begun a good work in you will complete it…" (Philippians 1:6).

"Father to the fatherless, defender of widows—
this is God, whose dwelling is holy."
(Psalm. 68:5, NLT)

2

WHIFFLE BALL

It was another summer's day during yet another summer vacation. This was the absolute best time of year as a child, except for Christmas time, of course. With school out and the sun in the sky, that meant it was time for baseball! Any kind of baseball... Little League, sandlot pick-up games, stoopball, stickball, curb-ball, you name it. Some days we played them all. But, when it was just my buddy, Vic, and me, it was whiffle ball. You know, the plastic ball with holes on one side (if it was official) and the plastic bat. Vic lived a few blocks from me—two blocks up and one block over.

It was an amazing time in our lives. We would play ball from the time we awoke in the morning until darkness interrupted our ability to continue. And, even then, we would try to set up some type of lighting to enable us to keep playing past sundown. That is, until our moms would call us in or it was time to watch the Yankee game on TV.

The only catch was that we were not permitted to participate in whatever fun we had planned for the day until our chores were done, so I learned to work quickly. As my younger brother, Paul, came of age to also be responsible for some of the chores around our home, he was added to my crew of one. At first, I considered him an asset, as utilizing an extra set of hands should enable us to complete our chores faster, thus allowing me to attend to the more important activities, like baseball. Dad did increase the daily work load a bit, but employing our joint efforts should still provide a more efficient outcome, or so I thought.

There was one problem, however. Paul's work ethic was apparently different than mine. I realized that he was only five or six but, still, his slow pace irked me. *How hard is it to pull a few weeds from the flower beds!?* He was constantly being distracted by an earthworm he discovered, or inquiring for the thousandth time, "Is this a weed?"

Much to my chagrin, I wasn't permitted to join my friends until we were BOTH done. This was a dilemma. Being an industrious lad, I determined that if I wanted to join my comrades as quickly as possible, all I needed to do was assist Paul to complete his chores. So, once I finished my share, I picked up at whatever point Paul was at and polished his off, too. After a while, though, one thing I noticed was every day it seemed Paul did a little bit less and I did a little bit more. (Did I mention that Paul was the brainy one and also the better ball player? But that's another story. . .)

Chores done, we were ready to play whiffle ball. It was a real sport to us and as such there were clearly defined rules, what we called "ground rules." The ground rules varied, depending on whether the game was to be played at Vic's house or mine. I resided on a fairly quiet block, as far as cars and traffic were concerned. Vic, on the other hand, lived on a very busy street. The basic ground rules were issued by the two commissioners of whiffle ball, better known as our moms, and were designed so we would not get run over by a passing vehicle.

At my place, the home field, the ground rules were easy. We employed one of those pitching practice nets, complete with a strike zone embedded in the netting that would allow the ball to spring back after it was thrown. This was our "catcher." Pitch the ball in the box and it was a strike. Home plate was at the top of the driveway.

The pitcher's mound stood at the end of the driveway where it met the road. The foul poles were the telephone pole (what some people called the utility pole), down the right field line, and the left edge of my neighbor's drive-way across the street for the left field line. The distance was approximately forty feet wide. Hit the ball past the pitcher on the ground anywhere on the street and it was a single. Hit the ball across the street to the narrow three feet of grass between the curb and the sidewalk, including the curb, and you had a double. Hit the sidewalk on a fly for a triple and onto the neighbor's lawn for a home run. Catch anything in the air for an out. Anything on the ground, as long as it didn't pass you, was also an out.

The "ballpark" at Vic's house was completely different. Due to the heavy traffic, it was not prudent to hit the ball onto the street. To prevent this, we moved home plate back to the inside and rear of Vic's garage, located at the rear of the property. Yes, I said "inside of the garage." The objective was to hit the ball out of the garage without hitting any part of the garage door frame, to be a fair ball.

Hitting line drives was the intended swing style. Doubles and triples were impossible but lining one over the small fence about halfway down his driveway was a home run. Vic did not own a net to utilize as our catcher, so we substituted an old wheelbarrow. By standing the wheelbarrow on its handle with the wheel up in the air, we created an acceptable catcher. If the pitch hit anywhere on the body of the wheelbarrow, what we called the "well," it was a strike. The strike zone was somewhat lower than the net at my house, but we justified this by applying more of a National League strike zone compared to the American League. (For those of us old enough to remember the American League umpires used a big pad on the outside of their clothing, preventing them from crouching as low as the National League guys, thus a slightly different strike zone.)

Before the game could commence, a team needed to be selected and it was required to know their starting lineups. Both Vic and I would argue as to who would represent the Yankees, both of us being avid fans, but we eventually worked it out. That would force one of us to select another team, like Baltimore or St. Louis. The key was that you had to mimic each player when batting. If they hit lefty, you had to hit lefty. If they were righty, you had to swing from the right side. We even attempted to copy their mannerisms. How they approached the plate. How they held the bat. Open stance or closed stance. We studied each player.

I throw from the right side. Vic was a southpaw. The batter was also the announcer, providing current player stats and calling balls and strikes. We even tried to imitate the announcers. He was Phil "Holy Cow" Rizzuto. I was Mel Allen, "How about that!" You couldn't tell the players without a program. And even then . . .

"Play Ball!"

Afterthought: The Gift of Brotherhood

Vic and I have known each other since we were about twelve years old; we went to school together, were each other's "best man," and are still good friends after these fifty-five years.

Brotherhood or sisterhood is a special gift. I hope you have good friends in life. The counterpart to the value of *having* a good friend is the value of *being* a good friend. Frankly, I believe you need to be a friend before the gift of friendship is bestowed on you.

Brotherhood is extremely essential to a man. This type of relationship is vital if a man is to fully develop and mature as God intends. That's the key phrase... *as God intends*. Our culture attempts to define the attributes of manhood and often, I believe, misses it in many ways. Our ethos labors to convince men that they must be independent, never show emotion, and accept all the pain that life can bring and smile as it brings it. To "go it alone" rather than link arms with other men. To never ask for directions or help or a hand up... never! That is, if we are "real men."

But that is not how we are designed by our Creator. He said, "It is not good for man to be alone." The Almighty has set a high value on companionship, including friendship and brotherhood, associating the greatest of all love with the giving of one's life for his friend (John 15:13).

The story of David before he was king and the friendship he had with Jonathan, King Saul's son, illustrates loyalty and brotherhood that withstood the pressure of the day. I encourage you to look it up in a Bible (see 1 Samuel 20) and read some of their story for yourself, for your own encouragement. You can also read about how even Almighty God befriended Abraham, accrediting his faith as righteousness. Imagine, having that title attached to your accolades... a friend of God (James 2:23).

I am blessed with a number of men who have chosen to walk alongside me. And, I have the privilege to stand with them in their lives. Together we find strength, encouragement, wisdom, perception, and truth. At times, admonishment, but always love. I have heard it said that the value of a man is found in the number of his friends. I pray you develop many.

> *"Let love be without hypocrisy. Above what is evil.*
> *Cling to what is good. Be kindly affectionate*
> *to one another with brotherly love, in honor*
> *giving preference to one another."*
> (Romans 12:9-10)

3

T-BALL, WHAT'S T-BALL?

I was finally eight years old and eligible to join Little League. The initial age group was the "Farm League" for the youngest of us boys. Some may know this as the Pee-Wee League or T-Ball.

I was a star at T-Ball! Then again, we all were. Each of us had opportunity to play all the positions and it seemed that no matter where you hit the ball it was a home run—not the majestic blast that allows the batter to trot around the bases at a celebratory gait, but that "swing-with-all-your-might" squib to second.

This was also my initiation to having my first coach other than my Dad. Mr. Vella was my friend Tommy's dad. He was the manager of our little baseball team, but he taught us much more than the fundamentals of baseball, especially as we grew into our teenage years. I was fortunate to have Mr. Vella as my coach through most of high school as well. Learning about sportsmanship, fair play, how to lose gracefully, and how to win honorably were all on the lesson plan. He taught us how to support our teammates, and bring a positive attitude each and every day, even when we were on the bench. When we made an error or some other mental blunder, he was quick to bring correction, but to teach, not to reprimand—he always encouraged us to improve. There were more lessons than simply baseball rudiments, some I didn't catch until I was an adult myself. Things like patience—a definite requirement when dealing with fifteen or so eight-year-olds, perseverance—to work through the practice time to prepare for the real game, teamwork—that it is about the team's success, not just the individual's, and the art of winning—how to win in all endeavors through hard work, endurance, failure and practice, appreciating one's teammates, and staying humble while, at the same time, standing tall.

There was equal parts fun memories to go along with the life lessons, of course. I even recall the events of my inaugural T-Ball experience. It was my first time at bat, and I swung as hard as I could, hitting a ground ball that barely reached the kid on second base. I ran with all I had toward first base as the errant throw soared over the first baseman's head, triggering my coach, manager, and every sideline parent rooting for our team to yell, "Go to second, go to second!" As I made sure I touched first base, landing squarely in the center of the base with both feet, I continued to advance to second. I awaited the "SAFE!" call from the umpire-of-the-day, normally one of the other dads coerced into service. Instead, against the desperate cries from the opponent's coaches to "run it in," I saw the thrown ball sailing into left field.

"Should I stay, or should I go?" I asked my manager, a confused look on my face.

"Run!" rang out the instructive cries from the bench. So off I went—around third base, headed for home as fast as my young legs would carry me. Then, with an artistic slide into home, even though the ball was still being retrieved by the left fielder, I was "SAFE!" It was a home run. Dad was so proud. My manager was exhaustively pleased, too.

I was sure I had been instructed at some time to always slide into home plate. So, slide I did! After the game, I had the proof I needed. My tiny uniform was filthy from the game-deciding slide. My brother and sister, and especially my mom would certainly be convinced that I *actually* played in the game. Final score: 28-27—we won! Thank you, Coach!

Afterthought:
The Battles We Face

Life is filled with battles, challenges, and choices we need to make. How we face them is determined by the lessons we receive, the truth presented, and the outcomes of those events. Unfortunately, many of us so often hear, "You can't, you won't, you'll never . . ." either from others or our own self-doubt. Labels start to attach themselves to our identity, molding our anticipated result towards failure more than success.

Each of us is created to win, to be victorious. Think about it. We always feel great when we win, especially after a gallant effort. It seems right when we win. All throughout the Old and New Testaments in the Bible, we see individuals who were obedient to God be victorious, winning their battles. These are examples for us to follow, coaching, in a way. It is indeed God's desire that we overcome the trials, challenges, and battles we face throughout life, that we stand in the winner's circle and receive the trophy or gold medal. From the time we are children we learn to play, to share our toys, to be part of a team, to accept the outcome of the "game," win or lose. But, let's be honest . . . we want to win!

The real prize is not the award or the cash prize, but who we become through the battle, though the experiences in life. Identity is established by the creator, designer, architect of an object. The manufacturer decides what an object is and what its purpose is. We are no different. God has created a magnificent entity in the human being and implanted in us the abilities to learn, reason, make choices, experience, and develop. The intent is that we would grow in every aspect . . . "That you may prosper in all things and be in health, as your soul prospers." (3 John 1:2)

Our character is not defined by whether we win or lose. We can, and should, learn much from either result. Our character is determined by our virtuous and honorable effort. "Did I do my best today?" When we are young, these experiences prepare us for the bigger ordeals life inevitably brings our way. Do we take each battle and utilize its lessons as the young shepherd boy David did, leaning on his experience fighting the lion and the bear to defeat Goliath? Or, do we shrink back, avoiding these difficulties with a distraction permitting us to hide from the possibility of failure?

It is not too late for us! The cast is not set! We *can* be all that God intended, regardless of our past. We just need to relearn who we are and whose we are. As the Apostle Paul famously said, "When I was a child, I spoke as a child, I understood as a child; but when I became a man, I put away childish things" (1 Corinthians 13:11).

Real life is not T-Ball. It is hard, demanding, and unforgiving most of the time, with harsh consequences. But that doesn't mean we can't win. God provides us teachers, coaches and mentors to show us the way. We can prepare, train, and practice in the matters of God, and muster all the strength we can to apply all the tools, weapons, and know-how He provides.

May we walk as mighty men of valor, mighty men of God, and face the battle, overcome the fear, and gain the victory—not by our own hand but by leaning and depending on the One who truly has our back. Yes, if God is for us, who can be against us? Our source of strength is in expending our efforts and in the grace of God who makes up for our shortcomings. We are not expected to be perfect, but we are expected to give an effort of excellence!

To the one who is victorious, I will give the right to
sit with me on my throne, just as I was victorious
and sat down with my Father on his throne.
(Revelation 3:21, NIV)

4

T-BALL IS OVER —A TRIBUTE TO TED

About midway through the Farm League season, I showed up to the field to discover we would not be utilizing the "T" anymore. It was time to pitch and hit.

"I am ready!" I declared to myself.

The first question our manager needed to determine was who could pitch. We all volunteered. Our manager selected two or three of us and brought us into foul territory to warm up. I understand now that our manager was just trying to locate someone, anyone, who could throw relatively straight and had the ability to reach home plate. Our catcher was Tommy. He was the heftiest of us, to put it kindly. I remember thinking, *He won't even need any of that padding,* but he was required to wear it anyway.

Then it was time to set the lineup. I remember being pleased, thinking, *Wow, I'm playing second base and batting fourth. The best hitter on the team's position in the lineup. Could it be that my manager recognizes my talent already?* It never occurred to me that he just had us hitting by fielding position, one through nine. Second base, universally identified as the "four-hole," was simply fourth on the lineup card. I do not recall how I did in the field that day, but my guess is not very well, for I was in left field the next game. *Anything but right field*, my ego shouted inside. The worst kid always played right field.

I do remember the first time I stepped up to the plate to face a pitcher. I walked up to the plate imitating to the best of my ability, my baseball idol, Mickey Mantle. I assumed my batting stance and leered out toward the pitcher with a glare of grit and determination that would intimidate even Sandy Kofax. My opponent looked in to get the sign. (We did not use signs yet, but that is what you do when pitching.) He took his windup and let it fly. "Strike one!" bellowed the ump.

I recollect wondering, *Why is the ump standing behind the pitcher? That's not where they stand on TV? Okay, Dennis, focus.* As I prepared for the next pitch, I reminded myself, *I have to swing this time.* Again, I took my stance, even more determined, to swing and hit the ball.

"Strike two!"

Again, I amazed even myself. *Why didn't I swing? It was right down the middle.* I glanced at my coach.

"It just takes one!" he yelled as encouragement.

"Right," I agreed "It just takes one! I'm gonna swing this time and hit the ball into outer space!"

The pitcher wound up and threw the ball. "Strike three!" came the call. My heart sank.

I'm out? How could I be out? My first real hitting debut and I didn't swing. Not once.

"You'll get 'em next time," my manager said encouragingly, as I came back to the bench, devastated.

My first season did not unfold how I envisioned it at all. I think I was on base once the entire season—and even then, I walked. The rest of the time I struck out. Most of the time without swinging. Oh, and I also played right field.

The next two years were not much better. I still couldn't hit, rarely swung, and was a permanent figure in ... you guessed it, right field. But, I never gave up; I just loved baseball too much.

Dad and I played catch often and he encouraged me to swing the bat. "You will never hit the ball if you don't swing," he would say, always with an encouraging tone, to help me believe that what he said was true. "Don't be afraid of the ball." I still rarely swung. Then, one day it happened. I got hit with a pitch and I realized that it really didn't hurt that much. Truth is, a ten-year-old kid doesn't throw very hard. As we matured, it hurt much more.

After that first time, I realized I did not have to be afraid of being hit by the pitch. Victory at last! I made up my mind and set my resolve. *I am going to swing at the first pitch the next time I am at the plate.* Next time up, on the initial pitch, I swung with all my might. My eyes were still closed a bit, but it happened … I hit the ball, or maybe the ball hit the bat. It didn't matter. I had my first hit! From then on, I began to swing—mostly with my eyes closed, but I was swinging. "Keep your eye on the ball," I heard from all the dads, coaches, the manager, and even the moms. How embarrassing. But I was swinging. That was the important thing. I would never hit the ball unless I was willing to swing. I was swinging!

I was never an adequate hitter through my elementary and teen years. I was always around the "Mendoza" line until I began to understand the science and the proper approach to hitting. (For those not aware, the Mendoza line, named after Mario Mendoza, was a batting average of .200—not good.) I owe this understanding to an article I read in *Sports Illustrated.* It was written by the late, great Ted Williams.

Now, as an avid Yankee fan, and specifically a Mickey Mantle fan, Boston's Ted Williams was not real high on my list of favorite ball players. But, sometimes greatness transcends the boundaries of rivalry. Ted Williams was a great hitter and the last professional baseball player to hit .400 for an entire Major League season. Even I figured out that I could learn something regarding hitting from him. And learn I did. Ted explained via this article the science of batting: concepts like understanding the hitting zone, how to be selective with what you swing at, how to recognize a fastball from a curveball, what type of pitch to look for in different pitch counts and situations, how to stand at the plate, how to grip the bat, how to swing, and everything else you could possibly hope to learn about hitting. It was an amazing article.

I began to "see the ball" as Mr. Williams taught for the first time in my still-young baseball career. I was fourteen or so and playing in what they called the "Pony league." This was the league for thirteen and fourteen-year-old boys. The Colt League was for fifteen through sixteen and Connie Mack was seventeen and eighteen-year-olds. The first full season after I read, practiced, and applied what I learned from this article, I led the league in hitting. No kidding! I was amazing! From that time on, I batted over or around .300. No more Mendoza line for me.

I didn't play past the age of eighteen, but I did learn how to hit and that I owe to Ted. That article was transformational—a master sharing his knowledge with whomever would receive it. Miraculous. Imagine, me as a young boy, reading. That was a miracle in itself. And, as my dad would say, "Apply what you learn." He was all about action! Thank you, Mr. Williams.

And one more thing: I didn't play right field anymore, either.

Afterthought: Wisdom Is Applied Knowledge

Knowledge is a great thing to obtain, as it establishes understanding. Applied knowledge is greater still, as it authenticates the acquired information through action. Proof of one's personal experience provides a truth that endures, which is referred to as "wisdom."

Wisdom benefits a person's life and the lives of those around him. God has furnished us a miraculous and wondrous brain, enabling us to think, reason, recall, and create. He imparted to us not just a brain, but what the Good Book describes as a "sound mind" (2 Timothy 1:7), permitting us to not just think, but to think correctly. This is a learned and practiced skill. Yes, He has bestowed upon us the ability, but it is up to us to become effective thinkers, planners, and users of our brain power. I am not talking about becoming an Einstein-level genius. I AM talking about making good life choices, about having God's mindset and perspective. The adage of "garbage in, garbage out" is not limited to the computer, tablet, and smart phone in your possession. It begins with that area between the two ears God gave us. I believe God's wisdom is far above the insight, judgement, and intelligence of man and our culture.

We all know men who consistently seem to make bad choices. We would all have a plethora of examples if we were to focus on our own lives, but it is much easier to recognize this behavior in someone else. Even those who are highly educated can fall into this category, so perhaps education on its own is not the answer. Personal experience may be a better teacher, but true wisdom and applied knowledge are key.

Proverbs 4:7 says, "Wisdom *is* the principal thing; *therefore* get wisdom. And in all your getting, get understanding." God's Word encourages us to seek wisdom, to "get" wisdom. And in all that "getting," to learn, embrace, acquire, and understand so we may *apply it*—to make good choices, to succeed at a task (or at life itself). Maybe even to simply improve at baseball! Really, God knows everything about everything. And He provides, so be grateful and appreciate your teachers, mentors, and coaches, and especially appreciate the Big Guy upstairs!

> *"I will instruct you and teach you in the way you*
> *should go. I will guide you with my eye."*
> (Psalm 32:8)

5

A MOUSE IN THE HOUSE

Memories are a fantastic gift from God. Have you ever thought about that? Some are momentously impactful, and others rather insignificant, yet they are there burned into our memory bank all the same. This is a memory of the latter—seemingly an insignificant part of my life, but to this very day, there it is. Isn't that amazing! I love when God "wows" us with something like this and I would hope you have some of these, too.

On a cool, rainy day, I was home from school on a holiday break—Thanksgiving, I believe. I was maybe eight at the time and, as would be a normal occurrence on a gloomy day, hanging out in my room playing and trying not to wake my baby brother. We shared a room and I quickly learned that if Paul didn't take his nap, he would be much more difficult to deal with. I loved the little guy. He wasn't as much fun as a puppy, but he was pretty cool as long as he didn't spit up on me, or worse.

Anyway, on this particular day I had also fallen asleep for a quick nap. I despised sleeping during the day as I was sure I would miss something, and this day proved my point.

As I opened and rubbed my eyes from my midday snooze, making sure I didn't awaken Paul, I wandered down the hall to find my mom sitting in the den with the TV on. Mom never watched TV in the daytime, so this struck me as a bit strange. She seemed pretty involved with what she was watching. She had an intense focus, barely noticing my entrance into the room.

"What are you watching, mom?" I asked. "Shushhh-hhh," she replied, "There's a mouse in the house." *Ohhh*, was my silent response. It must be a comedy. No! A mystery! That's it, a good whodunnit. Mom always enjoyed a good mystery. Charlie Chan, Sherlock Holmes, the Eastside Kids. Then she delivered the actual revelation. "No, Dennis. There is a mouse in the house! I heard some little noises and then spotted him running across the floor."

What? An actual mouse! You saw it?! I knew I shouldn't have taken a nap! I retrieved the broom to use as my armament. Now, the hunt was on. Not under the couch, nor behind the TV stand. "Don't worry, Mom," I tried to assure her. "I'll rid us of this rodent offender." But, it was not behind the big plant in the corner by the stairs.

Not in the radiator. Nothing. I couldn't unearth his hiding place anywhere.

"I think he went into the baseboard radiator pipes," I reported with a tone of failure and remorse, as I had wanted to come through and save the day. When Dad wasn't at home I was the "man of the house." Yeah, sure, a man or a mouse. This time the mouse won.

"Wait for your father to come home from work. He'll trap him," Mom said. Dad was always saving the day. Whether a little mouse or something more dangerous, he always made us feel safe. He always protected us. Next time . . . this little rodent would be mine!

Afterthought: A Father's Covering

Yes, memories are fantastic gifts from God, even those seemingly without impact. But are they really trivial and immaterial? The fact that we recall such events must represent something of importance; otherwise, why reserve the real estate in our brains? A great part of this ability is the imagery of our memories and the deeper values they instill. As we recall the images, we also recall the emotion of the moment.

For me, I would have to say that I recognized and aspired to provide the same protection to my family as my father demonstrated time and time again. No dragons, mind you. Just a real sense of safety, security, solving problems, and doing whatever he needed to do in order to provide for his family. That's a Dad's job. Today, it is often a Mom's job, too.

The creation of a "covering" is something God initiated and continues to provide. We as men and fathers are to provide this same environment for those placed in our care. I had a good mentor in my dad, but not all men have good examples. Some have no example at all. Whatever the examples in one's life, the responsibility of caretaker remains.

It is a man's responsibility under the statutes of Heaven to prove, provide, and protect his family just as God proves, provides, and protects him. "Follow me as I follow Christ," (1 Cor 11:1, MEV) as stated by the Apostle Paul, is a good biblical example of this attitude.

It is a man's duty to establish and maintain order in the home—not merely by his command nor his hand, but by the time he spends on his knees in prayer. Men's pastor Scott Caesar has aptly said, "When a man is out of place, his wife is misplaced, his children are displaced, and God is replaced." I agree!

The question we must ask ourselves is, "Are we providing the covering that God has charged us to provide?" Do we know how? Do we know and depend upon the One who does? Will we learn, practice, and execute?

> *"He who dwells in the secret place of the Most High shall abide under the shadow of the almighty. I will say of the Lord, He is my refuge and my fortress; My God, in Him I will trust."*
> (Psalm 91:1-2)

6

THE AGONY OF CHRISTMAS EVE

nticipation. I have come to realize this is not a word I embody naturally. It is a two-sided coin, neither side of which I am fond of. It doesn't matter if it is the anticipation of a bad thing, like bringing home a poor report card from school and waiting for the lecture from mom and dad, or the anticipation of a good thing, like having to sit at the dinner table when Mom has made one of your favorite meals and you can't dig in until everyone sits at the table and gives thanks. "Come on, where is everybody? Time to eat! I'm gonna die from hunger. Aaahhh!" Either way, anticipation is not something I handle well. Maybe you feel the same.

It's the pain of delay, the discomfort of patience, the agony of the wait that I find unbearable. The waiting "until your father gets home," as Mom would threaten, was always worse than a quick slap on the bottom. My mind would go wild with crazy ideas as to what would happen. *What will Dad do? Will I get corporal punishment with a spanking? Grounded for the rest of my life? Maybe hard labor with some horrible chore?* Conceivably, I broke the "last straw" and he will kill me and bury me in the backyard?" Yes, the anticipation was, and always is, unbearable. Anticipation of a "bad" thing brought me dread. Anticipation of a "good" thing generated a euphoric sense of excitement almost too great to bear. I get excited about everything. I even find excitement seeing others get excited.

So, what does this have to do with Christmas, you ask? Christmas is a wonderful time. It's my favorite holiday season—always was, and still is, but the anticipation of Christmas morning in my younger years was almost unbearable.

I am the eldest of three children and thus the benefactor of some early family traditions that were equal parts ridiculous and whimsical. The magic in my house growing up was amazing. How my parents pulled it off was an absolute mystery and it fueled my level of excitement to the nuclear level.

For example, Christmas Eve when I was five was nothing special. For the most part, it was just another night. The outside of the house was slightly decorated with lights and there were some small pieces of holiday decor around the inside, but there was no Christmas tree, no wrapped presents, and no stockings hanging on the mantel.

Then, by Christmas morning, somehow it was all transformed. The Christmas tree magically appeared, decorated immaculately. The effect was breathtaking, down to the tinsel, each branch glistening with the reflection of the lights. This was a tedious job as each strand of tinsel needed to be placed perfectly on each branch, one strand at a time. The lights were lit, and ornaments glimmered and sparkled. Stockings were in place, all stuffed with small gifts. Presents were under the tree, wrapped with beautiful colors and ribbons (all about to be ripped into pieces). A true Christmas wonderment…. and all done in one night by "Santa" while I slept. Magical. Absolutely magical. What anticipation! But oh, so hard to … wait.

Next memory: I am now eleven or twelve years of age. The rules in our house for us kids were that we could not leave our rooms Christmas morning until we were all awake and "not before 7:00 a.m." I was able to negotiate a 6:00 a.m. time with Dad, as he received the authoritative nod from Mom, the official time keeper, but we ALL had to be awake. I thought I worked out a great deal on the 6:00 a.m. thing, for who could sleep with all the excitement? I never would have thought that my younger sister and brother would be the ones to betray me.

I hardly slept a wink, being fully awake by 4:00 a.m. as I began preparing for our onslaught on the gifts, where I would lead our tiny squadron of bandits to feast on the treasures under the tree. With my commando mindset fully engaged, I synchronized my watch with the clock in my room. Only two hours till C-DAY! (Christmas Day). *But wait, what's that sound?* Soft snoring sounds from my two compadres. *What are they doing? Why aren't they awake, at least stirring?* I check my watch; it reads 4:11a.m. *Still sleeping?! Where's their passion? Fortitude? Commitment to the task?*

Have you ever noticed that the time from when you fall asleep until the time you wake up seems to go in a snap? It is my observation that one has no concept of time while asleep. Think about it. It's true! One moment you are drifting off to sleep and then, "POW," you're awake and six or eight hours has gone by. This phenomenon was something I was acutely aware of, and adopted as my primary strategy. *Once I go to sleep... the next moment will be morning.* Suitable approach for handling the anticipation, right? That was my logic. Early to bed and the morning would arrive in a snap.

So, applying this logic, why not go to bed a bit earlier? Great idea! 4:00 p.m.? Time for bed! "Not hungry, Mom, just exhausted," I declared as I retired to my room. Only one issue: I was wide awake! Not only was it still daytime, I was jacked with excitement and expectations for the next day. Who could sleep? No wonder I was up by 4:00 a.m. What agony!

By 5:30 a.m., my sister was finally stirring. I admit I generated a little noise, threw stuff at her, shook her bed (all without alerting my parents, of course), but what about the little guy? Paul was out cold. Worse yet, he wasn't one to get too amped up about anything. He had absolutely no trouble sleeping soundly, despite my mischief. Another agonizing fifteen minutes crept past and still no movement from my brother. *Doesn't he know the assault is scheduled for 0600 hours?*

"A little more patience, Dennis; we are getting close," I told myself. My sister and I passed the last few minutes before CDAY playing a quick card game of Go Fish. Connie won. I really did not care as I offered the excuse of being distracted.

After the game, I checked the clock once more, unable to keep my eyes off it for long . . . 6:05?? How can it be 6:05? I looked at my brother and he was still asleep. Asleep! He was thwarting the plan. After all, I negotiated, "Six a.m., no earlier, but you can't wake each other." This was a caveat I hadn't planned for. I rechecked my synchronized watch—6:18. *This is insane! How can he still be sleeping?* The waiting was agony and, as far as I was concerned, completely unnecessary. Time for intervention.

I returned to my parent's room. It was precisely 6:22. "Hey, Dad?" I said softly, so as not to startle him. "Connie and I are awake. I think Paul is dead. Can we go down to the tree?"

He said, "No," and sent me back to my room. Sigh. The caveat to my plan successfully prevented the onslaught and dismantled a perfect plot.

"This is agony! Agony!" I wailed, as I disappeared back into my room and my despair. By the way, Paul didn't wake up till 7:00 a.m. So much for my negotiation skills.

Afterthought:
Patience Is a Virtue

Patience is such a difficult quality to master. Most of the time the "what" we are waiting for, as well as the "how" we are waiting, dictates the pressure we feel when we are required to exercise patience.

When we ask, "What's for dinner?" directly after finishing lunch, simply because we are curious as to what will be the next meal, does not require much patience. But, if you were one of the thirty-three men trapped in the San Juan mine in Chile for 69 days, waiting your turn to be rescued, it would be a very different story.

I often wonder if God wants us anticipating, planning, and projecting things in life. We all want good success and good health, and we must organize, prepare, and make ready those issues to accommodate our well-being. God is a God of order, and He wants us to also be in order. But sometimes our planning and anticipation of our future life dealings can cause us to be anxious. I agree that faith is the substance of the unseen and we must have faith that our Father in Heaven will supply all that we need. In a way, faith is "anticipating" the provision God says He will provide. Jesus also said that we should not worry about tomorrow, for tomorrow will worry about itself (Matthew 6:34). Well, which is it?

I believe God wants us to practice patience. To take advantage of the opportune time to receive the absolute best outcome and to develop an unsurpassed godly character. Not to focus on the desired provision, life event, or life condition outcomes, but to focus on the majestic entity from which the need or outcome will be provided. Not the gift, but the Giver.

Yes, patience is a virtue—meaning a "high moral standard" or a "good and useful quality" of something. We are instructed to have faith and to add moral standards to that faith (2 Peter 1:5-11, ESV). This passage continues on to say we must add knowledge, self-control, and then patience, all of which lead to godliness and then to brotherly kindness and love. Patience seems important in building the character of a man.

I've heard it stated that often we pray to God for patience and then ask Him to hurry in providing it. Think of the other words related to patience, such as endurance, fortitude, resolve, persistence, perseverance, and tenacity. These are the qualities of virtue we are to walk in. We can do it, but we need to transform into God's guys, God's people.

Isaiah 40:31 says, "But those who wait on the Lord shall renew their strength; they shall mount up with wings like eagles, they shall run and not be weary, they shall walk and not faint."

"Wait on the Lord" is the prerequisite. "Shall run and not be weary" is the promise. Our Great, Great Father would not affirm the virtues of the character He would want us to possess and not provide the wherewithal to obtain them.

Listen to these words of wisdom as they pertain to patience: "My brethren, count it all joy when you fall into various trials, knowing that the testing of your faith produces *patience*. But let *patience* have *its* perfect work, that you may be perfect and complete, lacking nothing" (James 1:2-8, emphasis added). *Exercise patience. That you may be matured, be perfected. Lacking nothing.* Isn't that what we all want?

> *"Be anxious for nothing, but in everything by*
> *prayer and supplication, with thanksgiving, let*
> *your requests be known to God."*
> (Philippians 4:6)

7

BOXING LESSONS

My dad is a gentle man, yet a strong man. He will "bend" on those less important issues that so many of us take a hard position on. We fight to be right, to be heard, to influence the other guy on stuff that really doesn't matter. Dad can also be incredibly strong when it comes to those things that are important, like principles, precepts, and promises. He understands what love is. Sacrificial love. He just turned ninety-five at the time of this writing, and I must say he has been one of the greatest gifts God has afforded me.

I am all too aware of the poverty of a man's soul that can occur when he has not been similarly blessed. In many families, there are situations where there is strife, bad behavior, taking advantage of others, lies, theft, and, well, the list can be long. In many of these cases, it is not unusual for relationships to break down. Unconditional love, on the other hand, says, "I love you," even when we are at our ugliest. This I learned from the man I call "Dad."

He would not allow us to construct excuses for our failures. Instead, he utilized these occasions as teaching moments—not in the method of sitting us down and explaining, necessarily, but more often with some type of "character building" life lesson he had learned and lived himself.

I remember a time, I believe I was twelve or thirteen, when I was being a bit bratty to my mom and giving her sass. This was a "no-no" in my house, as dad always taught us to respect others, not just Mom—although she was at the top of the list—but everyone, especially women. ("Honor your mother and father." I think I heard that somewhere. One of the big ten.) Well, on this day I did not honor her nor respect her. I was being fresh, difficult, and disrespectful. Even at that young age, I was aware that I had hurt her with my behavior. Normally, Mom would handle much of the discipline herself, as she had no trouble ruling the roost, but this day she didn't. I suppose whatever I said stung her deeply. We often forget how damaging and hurtful the sting of our words can be.

During dinner that evening (we always ate together as a family, something I highly recommend if you haven't dined together lately), Dad announced he thought it was time I was instructed in the art of boxing, and after dinner he would impart to me my first "lesson." *Cool,* I thought.

I always love spending time with Dad. No one mentioned anything about the situation with Mom earlier in the day. Mom seemed okay. Dinner was great, as usual. I figured she would let it slip by. No big deal. I had dodged the bullet.

Ah, the naiveté of youth. After dinner, we always helped clear the table. Dad said, "As soon as we're through helping Mom in the kitchen, we'll go into the garage, okay?" *This will be great!* I thought to myself, excitement building. Once in the garage, dad took down the two sets of boxing gloves. I wasn't aware we had them, as Dad didn't box, as far as I knew. I think my grandfather had boxed when he was young. He had referred to the Golden Gloves organization at different times. I had never given it much thought.

Dad placed the gloves on me and instructed me as to the correct ways of lacing them up. "Make sure they are good and tight, especially around your wrist." He showed me how to protect my thumb and not injure myself when throwing a punch. He coached me on how to deliver a jab, an upper cut, and how to use my body to add power to the punch. I was unaware Dad was such an expert on boxing! When it came to defense, he demonstrated how to move up and down, left and right. How to hold my hands up to protect my face and to keep my elbows in to protect my ribs and stomach. Wow, what a lesson!

Okay, time to spar. Now that I was aware of all the technique, I really wanted to spar with dad. "Com'on, Dad. Put up your dukes!" This is when reality occurred.

We began to box. Me jumping all over the place like a wild rabbit, throwing jabs. Dad blocking them with ease. It was right about at that point in our boxing match that he asked the question of the day. It was more of a statement than a question.

"So, I understand you were not behaving very well today, talking back and being fresh to Mom." I didn't get a chance to answer. All I experienced and heard was the "pop" of his jab to the brow of my head. It didn't hurt, just surprised the daylights out of me. My dad had just punched me in the head!

"Hold your hands up," he declared, "like I showed you." Pop, another blow. This time he punched the glove on my left hand as I held it higher to protect myself, only to have my own hand snap backwards into my own face. Again, more surprised than hurt. Dad then issued his teaching moment, explaining, "When you are disrespectful to Mom, or anyone, your words can be hurtful, much like being punched in the gut."

He was very serious, as he can be, when he feels strongly about something. In this case, what was most important was that I learned how to honor my mother . . . my father, too. He wanted me to understand how a man, a real man, is to treat others. How we are to regard and respect women.

As we spoke, I looked deeply in his eyes, as the situation required my complete attention. As he completed the "boxing lesson," he looked for my acknowledgement.

I confirmed my understanding and whispered in an apologetic tone that I was sorry.

He gave me a bear hug as he always did, told me that he loved me, and directed me to apologize to my mother. We never took out the boxing gloves again.

Afterthought: For Whom God Loves

"Spare the rod and spoil the child." An old adage, probably no longer politically correct in today's culture. I think we all understand that there has been and continues to be many unfortunate occurrences of child abuse, and protecting our children from abuse of all kinds is paramount for our society. That being said, finding effective, compassionate ways to provide needed discipline is a high calling for parents.

There are many experts that have studied the effects of various types of discipline utilized in the rearing of our children. Some methods have greater results, or more desirable results, than others, but the instruction of our youngsters as to right from wrong is still a fundamental necessity for all of mankind.

As a father, it is my desire that my heirs are mature, have a good understanding as to what is good and what is evil, and a sense of how to treat people. I would hope they are honest, generous, kind, and possess integrity. I believe most people would want the same for their kids. Even more so, this is the desire of our Heavenly Father and, I believe, He has provided wisdom and knowhow through His precepts.

In the majority of translations, the aforementioned adage from Proverbs actually says, "Whoever spares the rod hates their children . . . (Proverbs 13:24)." A strong warning. It is obvious that, according to the Bible, a child's discipline has its place in the rearing of that child. Proverbs 22:6 reads, "Train up a child in the way he should go and when he is old, he will not depart from it." The Message translation of the same verse states, "Point your kids in the right direction – when they're old they won't get lost."

Is it me or do many of our kids seems lost?

Raising children properly is one of the most difficult assignments we are tasked with fulfilling in our entire lives. Many times we are children ourselves birthing children, then we are expected to successfully navigate the nurturing responsibility of a parent. As a senior citizen, as defined by our culture, I will admit that the majority of the prayers I have sent up to heaven concern my kids, my feeling of parenting inadequacy, my request for strength, patience, wisdom, understanding, forbearance, endurance, answers to the unending barrage of questions, hope, and at times, the ability to resist acting on the threat, "I brought you into this world, I can take you out" (just kidding)!

I am so grateful my dad taught me to discipline with love and wisdom, not out of anger. God never disciplines out of anger (thank God!). He always corrects out of love and I'm thankful for that (see Psalm 103:8-14). I was once lost, but now I'm found—nurtured by a benevolent, compassionate, generous, and empathetic Father God.

So are you.

*"For whom the Lord loves He corrects,
just as a father the son in whom He delights."*
(Proverbs 3:12)

8

THE FIRST TURKEY?

Thanksgiving . . . I so enjoy this holiday, partially because it begins the holiday season leading up to Christmas, my favorite holiday as a youngster, especially all the food. Every dish was somebody's "must have!" They even prepared the favorite dishes of those no longer with us. "This was Uncle Louie's favorite. God rest his soul," they would say solemnly as they performed the sign of the cross. Over the years, the women of our family realized that we could never consume the amount of food prepared (and who had the time to create the vast cornucopia of all our favorite holiday foods, anyway?). Today, we still consume an incredible meal celebration, but there is no comparison as to the way it was. This is how I remember that magnificent feast.

The year was 1961. Roger Maris had just broken the Babe's single season home run record the previous summer, so I knew the men would have plenty to talk about. I was only seven, but I hung out with the men, listening to each conversation, enjoying each sermon of the "old days" and laughing whenever they laughed. I never understood the punch line of the jokes and stories as they were always delivered in Italian. I remember wondering, frustrated, *Why do they do that?! They tell the whole story in English and then the best line of the story is in another language. Very strange.*

If you haven't figured it out yet, I am Italian. Well, half Italian. My mom's Irish. Well, half Irish and part Slavic. I'm not sure what Slavic is, though. Can't find it on a map. No country named Slavic. Maybe it fell into the sea, like Atlantis. We never talk about anything Slavic. Sorry, I got sidetracked. As I said, I'm Italian!

Thanksgiving dinner was always held at Aunt Catherine and Uncle Anthony's apartment in Corona, Queens. My Great Grandma and Great Grandpa also resided there. They were in their late eighties. They were always kissing me. I didn't mind Great Grandma so much, except that she had to kiss every inch of my face, but Great Grandpa's kisses were painful. He had a full beard and it scratched like nobody's business. Like a wire brush. Neither of them spoke much English, except, "How'd you say?" as they rarely could find the correct English words . . . and then they would continue in Italian. I never knew what they were saying without it being translated and at age seven nobody really cared if I understood or not. It was like watching a foreign film without the subtitles.

One thing I remember about Great Grandpa was his hair. He had a full head of pure white hair. His beard, too. Not long, always trimmed. Looked a bit like old photographs of General Robert E. Lee. I never saw him when he wasn't wearing a tie. He often smoked a cigar. He loved his family, was proud of us all, and he would sit at the head of the table gazing at each one of us, pausing for seconds at a time as if taking a quick inventory of what we were to become in life. Maybe he was praying. I was only seven so, as with all the kids, he just thought we were beautiful. He died a few years later. Great Grandma lived to one hundred and two. I remember them quite fondly.

Our family gathering was always large, fifteen to twenty of us in an apartment. There was a TV in the apartment, but it was never on. This day was about family, *la familia,* and the time together was around the table—men at one end and the women at the other. The women cooked and served, spending most of the time in the kitchen where there was always laughter and chatter. Pop would spout out, "It sounds like a chicken coop in there!"

The libations were served by one of the men, usually my dad or my uncle. A taste of wine, just a sip, was allowed on special occasions. This always made me feel that I was one of the adults, one of the men. We never had a "kids" table. We were always included. Always accepted into the "pack." Lowest in the pecking order, but still part of the pack.

Then, it was time for the food. Actually, there wasn't any specific time for the food; it just appeared. Guests would arrive, greeting hugs and kisses exchanged, a welcome glass of something was provided, and we all started taking our seats around the table. Right to the table. Probably because there was no other place to sit as the entire apartment was filled with the huge table and chairs.

On the table was the antipasto: cheeses, salamis, prosciutto and melon, figs, dates, peppers (both hot and roasted), olives, bread, and of course, wine. This was the meal before the meal, course one, until everyone arrived and were "settled." Course two was soup. Chicken soup, what most people now refer to as Italian Wedding soup, with little, tiny meat balls. My cousins and I would always see who received the most meatballs. "Eighteen. I have eighteen!" my cousin Tom would declare.

"Get outta here, you always say eighteen. Where are they?" I would challenge. Tom and I were the two eldest of the kids.

"I already ate six," he would retort.

Course three was the pasta. Most of the time ravioli. Homemade, of course. Hundreds prepared and laid out on my aunt's bed. What a sight! *Where do they sleep?* I often thought. Then the main course. "Anthony, come carve the first turkey," Grandma would call out. My cousin Tom and I looked at each other incredulously. *The first turkey? How many people are coming?* I thought to myself. I was already stuffed, and we hadn't even had the turkey yet! Not to mention the stuffing, mashed potatoes, sweet potatoes, what seemed like dozens of vegetables, cranberry sauce, and gravy. Just amazing.

After dinner, the table was cleared except for the carcass of the *second turkey,* which, at that time, was barely touched. The men played cards and told stories. Reminiscing stories. "Hey George, do you remember that 1937 Buick Pop bought off that guy from Brooklyn? ..." and so on.

I loved hearing of the days when my dad was a kid. My grandfather always told great stories, too, but not just something from the old neighborhood; usually it was some historical event that somehow came up in conversation. "George Washington crossing the Delaware? Oh yeah, I remember that. It was a cold winter night. I was there and I remember thinking, *Why don't we wait till the sun comes up?* But no, George needs to go right away. But the worst thing is that he always wanted to stand in the boat. I said, 'George! Sit down, you're rocking the boat.' True story, I was there." Pop told great stories and we kids believed every word.

While the cards were being dealt and the kids played dominos or some other games, a bowl of fruit and nuts, fresh figs, and dates always appeared on the table like magic. Cookies, cakes, pies, and pastries, too. Coffee, espresso, anisette, and other cordials. What a spread. Uncle started singing and the whole family joined in. Laughing so hard tears would flow from your eyes. I would get so full I could not imagine ever eating again. "Hey Julie," someone would call out, "bring out some bread in case someone wants a turkey sandwich."

A truly magical time of family . . . *la familia!*

Afterthought:
The Abundance of God

I have always found the Lord has shown me grace in many ways. One way I see His grace is in providing all that I need and then some. Sometimes in miraculous ways.

The Word of God, both Old and New Testaments, is filled with passages describing the abundance of God's provision: cattle on a thousand hills, roads of gold in heaven, blessing over blessing over blessing.

There are no strings attached to His blessing, but we are told there is a proper posture for receiving His blessing. For one, we are instructed to be generous, as He approves of such behavior, and rewards it. Second, we are to focus on the Provider, not the provision. Others include: to be obedient in honoring the Sabbath and the tithe. To balance the growth and well-being of spirit, body, and soul. To stay humble of heart, as it is His benevolence that rewards us. And to remember He is the rewarder of those who love and obey Him.

It is accurate to believe that our Heavenly Father knows all our needs and desires. He even pronounces that He "will give you the desires of your heart" (Psalm 37:4). However, God often ties a condition of the heart to His promises, as illustrated with the verse prior to this one: "Trust in the Lord, and do good; dwell in the land, and feed on His faithfulness. Delight yourself also in the Lord" (Psalm 37:3-4). And, in similar fashion, the verse after that says, "Commit your way to the Lord, trust also in Him, and He shall bring *it* to pass" (Psalm 37:5).

I have found that God's conditions, or desired "postures," are to mold our hearts towards Him, to enable us to receive the abundance He has for us. His love for us required Christ going to the cross and the grave, but His mighty nature and Master plan of redemption raised Him from the grave, and defeated death and all the works of the enemy of souls. This act of love and benevolence liberated us from bondage. If we can live in the postures—or conditions—God's Word sets forth, they provide us assurance that we will continue in His liberty, to live truly free. Galatians 5:1 avows, "Stand fast therefore in the liberty by which Christ has made us free, and do not be entangled again with a yoke of bondage."

Our entanglements come from out-of-balance desires: lust of the flesh, lust of the eyes, and pride (1 John 2:16). God's conditions keep our eyes on Him, keeps God first so we are not entrapped by selfishness, and sets us up to experience the abundant life He has for us—which is so much better than what the "world" has to offer!

There is no place in God's kingdom for greed, nor is there a place for lack. Trust God that He, and He alone, will provide all that you need, and then some. Delight yourself in Him, and He really will ABUNDANTLY provide the desires of your heart!

"Give away your life; you'll find life given back,
but not merely given back—given back with bonus
and blessing. Giving, not getting, is the way.
Generosity begets generosity."
(Luke 6:38, MSG)

9

PERGAMENT, POP, AND PETS

Back in the 1960s, there weren't any "big box" stores like Costco or Sam's Wholesale Club. We did have department stores, though, and if you needed any kind of home goods the place to shop was Pergament Home Center. They had just about everything.

As I recall, most Friday nights we, as a family, would trek out to purchase the supplies Dad would require for his weekend project. There was <u>always</u> a weekend project. Today, we want to get in, pick up what we need, and get out or, better yet, go online and have it delivered. But back then, it was not so. It was valuable family time, a family outing, another adventure, or so it seemed.

One observation I have made as times change is that the "core" family isn't so core anymore. As many of our children head off to college, all too often they don't return.

They pick a college somewhere you either have to fly to or plan a long weekend to get to. ("Road trip anyone?") They get an internship near their school, which turns into a job, they meet their significant other, and "BAM," they're gone. I'm not saying this is a bad thing, just an observation.

When my generation was growing up, at least in the New York City area and its suburbs, families lived close by. Grandparents, aunts and uncles, cousins—everyone was within thirty minutes of each other, if not down the block. Having a cousin who lived in another state, like New Jersey, was odd. They seemed liked outcasts or in the witness protection system (hmm, maybe they were). Visits to those out of state were only on holidays and it was always a hassle with the traffic and the tolls and the hour and a half drive. Someone was always complaining. The majority of us lived fairly close to one another. The "core family."

I thought it was great, as we were always getting together for something, even for something as common as a Friday night visit to Pergament's. Today, aunts and uncles and cousins are all "extended" family, often in more ways than one. Extended to reach to all parts of the country. Even the visit itself needs to be "extended" to now be several days, for it takes so long to get there. Now, we only see each other at weddings and funerals. I think it was better the old way. Just my opinion.

Back to Friday nights. On these nights, my grandparents on my mom's side would be at my house when I got home from school. Dinner was either pizza or Chinese food. I preferred pizza–Mom Chinese. Dad would bring home the goods on his way back from work and we would chow down quickly to enable us to get to the store. As I said, the whole family would go. Mom and dad, my little brother and sister, and Grandma and Pop. (That's what we called my grandfather.)

Pop was great. Not stuffy, down to earth. I remember he smoked non-filtered Chesterfield cigarettes and was always coughing his head off. Fair to say his health was not good as he got older and he passed in his seventies. What I remember most about him was that he did things his way, independent in every aspect. Most would consider him stubborn. I kind of liked that about him. Nobody was going to dictate to him what to do. Truth is, he should have heeded some of the advice he received as it would have benefitted him. Stubborn indeed.

For instance, he never trusted doctors. Would never go. Wouldn't even take the dog to the vet. Pups needing shots or needing to be dewormed… bah… he would give them a shot of whiskey, Irish whiskey, of course. That was Pop. Strong-minded and strong-willed. I found him very entertaining. My mother found him . . . stubborn.

My dad always had some around-the-house project he was working on. Whether building a retaining wall for a flower bed, putting up new wallpaper (mom was always changing the décor), or finishing the basement, there was always something.

Now, Pop was my mom's dad. He wasn't really that handy, at least not on the level acceptable to my dad. My Grandpa, on the other hand (that's what we called my grandfather on my dad's side), could handle just about anything. I guess it was natural for my dad to ask his dad for help. Thus, Saturday visits were from my other grandparents. My dad had to go to work on Saturdays, but Grandpa would get the project started and the two of them would work together on Sundays after church. I was usually the "gopher" for them. You know, "Dennis, go-pher some rags in the shed . . . go-pher the hammer in my toolbox . . . go-pher more nails in the garage."

I am blessed to have grown up with both sets of grandparents. In fact, I am blessed to be able to say that I knew my great grandparents on my father's side as well. I attribute this blessing to two major observations. There was no divorce in my family and they always lived what seemed to be a balanced life. No overindulgences (except maybe for Pop and his Chesterfields.)

And, we laughed a lot. I am proud to be able to say that when my daughter, Christy, was born, we had five generations living. A pretty rare and special occurrence as you need to live a long life to see four generations come after you. Christy, myself, Christy's grandfather (my dad), her great-grandmother, and her great-great-grandmother. When Christy's daughter, Emily, (my first granddaughter) was born, we repeated the feat again. Special indeed . . . "with long life does God satisfy" (Psalm 91:16).

Since Sunday was the only day Dad had off from his job, it was "his" day. Dad worked long and hard hours as an automobile mechanic. "Sunday is Dad's day," mom would announce. He would sleep in, if 8:00 a.m. could be considered sleeping in. I guess it is far better than the normal 5:00 a.m. A special breakfast, church, and then home. Mom always prepared a special Sunday dinner. More family time.

One of the things I remember about Sundays was that the stereo was off limits to us. Only Dad had access on Sunday. Dad loved his music: Glen Miller, Artie Shaw, Benny Goodman, the Dorsey Brothers, Sarah Vaughan, Sammy Davis Jr., and of course, Frank Sinatra. I never realized it then, but what an education I received of the music of the 1940s and 50s. Louis Prima, Ella Fitzgerald, Steve Lawrence and Eydie Gorme, Julius LaRosa, and the list goes on and on.

These were very special times and memories for me—all "happenings" in my life that are now part of me. I am so thankful for the legacy sown into me. Reflections of the men in my life. I suppose some would find me skilled enough to handle projects around the house like my grandpa. I do enjoy and appreciate an eclectic range of music genres like Dad. I'm not that fond of doctors. I love having my family together. I consider myself an independent thinker. I have a great love for God. And, some may see me as . . . a little stubborn. (Thanks, Pop.)

I also have a love for animals and that is something else Pop instilled in me on those trips to "Pergament's." You see, as Dad and Mom were shopping for whatever was necessary at the time, Pop would take me to the Pet Department. I guess that was the best way to keep a little kid occupied. Problem was, I always took great interest in what we discovered at the Pet Department and Pop was always looking to bless me. No matter how my mom threatened and warned Pop, "Do not to bring anything home," well . . . did I mention Pop was also independent and a little stubborn?

To my delight and pleasure, I often brought home some new pet. Nothing like a puppy, for you wouldn't purchase a puppy from a department store's pet department, but maybe a turtle, or a goldfish, or a lizard. I enjoyed them, but they never lived that long.

"Hey, Pop, how about an alligator?" (I had so much fun playing with my toy soldiers like a Godzilla movie.)

"They have rabbits!"

Or maybe it was baby ducks. (By the way, baby ducks grow into adult ducks, noisy ducks, as I found out to the disdain of my parents, whose bedroom was directly over the duck pen in the basement.)

"A hamster?" Why not, except the "boy" hamster was really a female, which had twelve baby hamsters. I can still hear my dad, "There are hamsters everywhere!"

"Hey Pop, I never had a snake." Problem solved.

"Don't tell your mother till we get home," he commanded.

Oh, yeah, he did eventually get me a puppy. His name was Lucky, and he was a beagle who loved to run. He was a great dog . . . most of the time.

"Dennis, Lucky got loose again!"

Afterthought: God Delights in You

It is my belief that God prefers communion, companionship, and sociability over isolation, seclusion, and loneliness. Genesis 2:18 tells us, "And the LORD God said, "*It is* not good that man should be alone."

Animals are wonderful no matter your favorite pet or form of wildlife; however, God's intent for us is to relate with other people. Interacting with one another, laughing, working, living together are all more enjoyable and healthier than being by oneself. It is a blessing to have friends and family, but all too often we engage in argument, distrust, and other selfish attitudes separating us from the very people we should be closest with. As the refrain goes, "You always hurt the one you love."

This scheme is one of the most effective weapons in the Enemy of Our Soul's arsenal. *Separate and conquer.* Our culture shouts, "You only live once," and, "Get all that you can." "Do unto the other guy before he does unto you," and, "What about me?" To think about me and mine and ignore you and yours. What a terrible way to live.

Sacrificial love, the highest form of love, demands we put others ahead of ourselves, especially when it comes to our family and friends. To extend ourselves to others. The Gospel of Luke, chapter six, refers to how we should treat and bless others and God's "boomerang" effect of blessings returning back to us, not just with an equal blessing but one of "good measure, pressed down, shaken together, and running over" (Luke 6:38). Most people believe this is related to one's generosity, but the verse just prior speaks of not judging others, not condemning others, and forgiving others as well. "For the same measure that you use, it will be measured back to you." Maybe there is more to generosity than money.

Friends and family will always disappoint, upset, frustrate, disagree with, and sadden us. We must recognize that this life is the training ground God has placed us in, so we may ascertain the ability to choose selflessness over selfishness. To elect not to record the wrongs of others rather than keeping score of every offence. To accept the idiosyncrasies and peculiarities of one another, rather than reject them through our biases, preferences, and prejudice.

Sure, there were conflicts in my family, like there are in all families. But I have the memories I have because, most of the time we tried to give each other grace. We forgave one another. We bore with one another. We celebrated one another, despite our differences and idiosyncrasies.

Whether you have a large family with several living generations as I do, or it's just you and your spouse, I encourage you to devote time to appreciate the specialness and sacredness of the gift you've been provided. You're assigned the task to either continue the wonderful heredity and family tree, or to start your own branch. To put down your own roots. To extend grace. To prioritize relationships.

Perhaps your family tree is only a sapling today, but with God's help, it can grow into a massive blessing. Twice in my life we have seen five living generations. WITH LONG LIFE He does satisfy.

"Delight yourself also in the Lord,
and He shall give you the desires of your heart."
(Psalm 37:4)

10

HIKING TO THE SEA

Have you ever had an idea that you thought was great, but turned out to be, well, let's say not so great, or not even good? In fact, what were you thinking? That was really stupid! This is such a memory.

It was the summer between the fourth and fifth grades. I guess that would make me about nine or ten. Summertime was great. No school, just fun, except for the few chores I had to do each day. Nothing but adventure.

There was no such thing as a "play date" back then, where Mom and/or Dad had to arrange a time and place to have fun. Not a time of chaperones. No video games, YouTube, smart phones, or home computers. Heck, we didn't even have the Internet. Nope, no Internet. Just good, unadulterated fun, outdoor fun. We never wanted to "stay in." If we were unable to recreate and play outside, it absolutely meant we were sick, or worse . . . grounded.

For me, my day started in similar fashion each day, except Sundays; there was church on Sundays. I would wake up, make my bed (I always had to make my bed), scarf down some breakfast, brush my teeth, do my chores, and then, "See ya, Mom; going to Paul's," (or Vic's or Brian's), and out the door. I could normally get away by 9:00 in the morning. No wastin' daylight for me!

Mom would yell, "Comb your hair before you go," but I was already out the door. I could never understand why I should comb my hair if it was only going to get messed up as I played. It's probably why I sported a crewcut from the time school recessed for summer break until I was back at school in September. I looked like a little Marine.

On this day, my friend Paul met me at my house and we decided to walk over to another friend's house to see what was happening there. Bruce lived just a few blocks away. We all were in the same class in the fourth grade. Bruce was always finding trouble in class or maybe trouble found him. Nothing horrible, but he would lose his concentration and disrupt the class somehow. (He probably had ADHD, but who had ever heard of Attention Deficit Hyperactivity Disorder before the 1980s?) We just thought of him as the kind of kid that was always inquiring why or how something worked. Inquisitive, always busy. He was an above average student in science, as was I, and that was our connection. Outside of that, not much in common.

Paul and I arrived at Bruce's house and found him outside in the driveway of his place. We did not have any particular plans for the day, which was probably our downfall. What do they say about idle hands being the devil's workshop (Proverbs 16:27, TLB)?

Bruce was not into playing sports as Paul and I were. Neither of us were into the taking apart of a radio that Bruce found in the garage to see why it was not operational, so we weren't sure what to do. "Hey, I've got an idea," Bruce suggested. "Why don't we go fishing at the reservoir? It's not very far. We can walk there!"

It sounded like an adventure to me, and I was always into adventure, although I didn't know what a "reservoir" was. "It's like a lake, stupid," Bruce informed me.

"Why didn't you just say 'lake'? I responded. "And where are we going to get the fishing poles?"

Well, Bruce had all kinds of stuff in his garage and we found one of those little plastic kid's poles amongst the piles and piles of boxes. You could barely walk or move your eyeballs, it was so packed. We engineered another fishing pole by spooling some tackle line on a stick. Now we were ready.

Trekking to the reservoir was not difficult direction wise. All you had to do was locate the little "stream," which actually started just behind our school, and walk south. So, off we went. The time was about 10:00 a.m. The genesis of our journey was easygoing, as there was no water in this section of the stream. It was more of a natural drainage brook about ten feet wide. I learned later, according to the EPA, it was the last active trout stream on Long Island. ("Trout stream? You're lucky to find a toad. Most of the time it is a dry as a bone!")

We walked and walked and finally came to a pool of water. "This isn't it," Bruce announced, "This is the first lake. We need to continue to the fifth lake. That's where the fish are." So, we continued. I picked up a walking stick, as I was always told you need a walking stick when hiking. I figured I could also use it if we came across any snakes, although I never spotted a snake anywhere in our neighborhood.

The stream south of the first lake had water, about two feet deep, but with the well-defined banks the hiking was still effortless. We had no idea as to how much time was passing by. We were just focused on our goal of reaching the fifth lake yet ahead of us. We came to several roadways with a fair amount of traffic. Most of the time we could hike under the overpass, but a couple of times we had to leave the bank of our stream and cross the road, returning to the stream bank on the other side. Onward past lake two, lake three, and lake four.

We were getting close to our destination, and the water way was getting wider and the ground around us was becoming more "swampy" in consistency. On several occasions, one of us slipped into the soft, wet, muddy ground. At one point, Paul lost a shoe in the mud and we needed to make a decision. Paul could either continue with the single shoe or we could leave him and pick him up on the way back. The crusade must not be thwarted. "I got it," Paul exclaimed, muddy shoe in hand, and we continued onward.

Unbeknown to us we had been walking for about three hours. None of us had thought to wear a watch, and we were completely unaware that we'd been walking for quite a while. "We must be close. I can smell salt water!" I declared. Suddenly, the wooded area of the stream opened up to reveal more of what resembled an inlet of the Great South Bay.

We attempted to locate a suitable place to fish but found ourselves standing in a marshy area with sea grass and some water lilies. To fish, you needed the ability to cast into the deeper water. The little kid's pole Bruce tried to utilize was not adequate, as he kept getting hung up in the weeds. I looked down at my "stick" with some tackle line and realized that I had no chance of catching a fish. On top of these disappointments, we all felt pretty dumb when Paul asked, "Who has the bait?" None of us had remembered the bait. It was at that moment that we grasped the reality that we had not only forgotten the bait, we also had also forgotten to inform anyone we were going fishing at the fifth lake!

We spotted a man fishing, surprising him when we appeared out from the marshy area like creatures from the Black Lagoon. "What are you kids doing here?" he asked. We explained our journey and inquired about the time.

When he said, "Almost 3:00 p.m.," we recognized that we were probably in trouble as we had a four-hour walk back. Our new fisherman friend laughed and said we'd better get a move on and get home. "Here," he said as we were leaving, offering three of the fish he had caught. "Better bring something home so your folks believe your amazing adventure story!"

Our journey back didn't take us as long and we made it in under three hours, as we knew we couldn't lollygag along the way. First stop, Bruce's house. You could hear his mom yelling at him from three blocks away. Just another ten minutes and Paul and I arrived at my house. Standing in front were both our moms. By the look on their faces, we could discern the fact that we were in trouble. It was 9:00 a.m. when we departed my place, returning nine and a half hours later – 6:30 p.m. "WHERE WERE YOU?" they bellowed in very distressed and upset mom voices. While I was being scolded, Paul's mom grabbed him by the ear and forcedly escorted him down the street, yelling something in Italian at him.

"But look, Mom," I interrupted showing her the fish. It was no consolation, and I would not pacify the wrath of Mom. At least we got home before the police found us. Oh yeah, Mom and Dad had called the police. That would add to my sentence.

The rest of the summer was very pleasant and uneventful. At least it seemed so from the view of my backyard, from which I was not permitted to vacate without adult supervision. I did learn to make very tight turns riding my bicycle in circles on the patio, though.

Afterthought:
Choose Ye This Day a Blessing or a Curse

As we grow and experience the matters of life, we hopefully make more good decisions than bad ones. With all of this, with all of life's affairs and experiences, we have the opportunity to learn. Life _is_ an adventure and, I believe, one in which we are to discover God and as much of His creation as possible. A great deal about God is discovered through His creation. Psalm 19:1, (NIV) states, "The heavens declare the glory of God; the skies proclaim the works of His hands."

Establishing boundaries – for right and wrong, good and bad, acceptable and unacceptable –

is what guides us in the choices we make. When we are children, our understanding and knowledge are limited to that which has been learned. Through this limitation, our decisions and selections display that lack of understanding, often resulting in unpleasant outcomes, such as, "Johnny, don't touch. It is hot."

As we mature, this basic concept does not substantially change. Our volume of learned views, beliefs, facts, and opinions—although a much larger body of work—still pilots us through the decision-making process. Our culture and ethos can greatly influence our worldview and the "truths" we accept and thus live by. What we seem to witness today is a greater dependence on the culture to establish one's worldview than faith-based ideologies. Could be a dangerous methodology.

I would suggest that the culture itself is influenced by the evolution of that same culture, creating somewhat of a moving target. How does one depend on the truth lessons of the culture when that same culture's truth is being defined and redefined by the modifications of that culture? Seems the dog is continually chasing its own tail. Where is the baseline? The plumb line? Without establishing a plumb line, a dependable base to measure thought, opinion, fact, and theory, how does one know what is actually true, real, or level?

For me, the answer is to really discover and learn about our Heavenly Father. Jesus defines everlasting life as "knowing God." Interesting definition. Everlasting life, that abundant life Jesus speaks of, is found in *"knowing God."* What a wonderful adventure He wants us to experience, with Him.

As we learn of Him, His truths are established within us. His plumb line, as He is the same yesterday, today and forever (Hebrews 13:8). Jesus said the reason He came was to "testify of the truth" (John 18:37, NIV). To testify one must witness. In effect, Jesus was saying that He was there when truth was established. He further claimed *He is* the Way, the Truth, and the Life (John 14:6).

The baseline of what is true and what isn't, the knowledge of good and evil, lies with getting to know God, especially if He is the Truth as he professes. What a marvelous discovery, if you can accept it. How impactful to one's life. There is only one truth. Perhaps that helps simplify some of the complexities of life. At least we can say the better

I know God, the more truth I will encounter, rather than trying to keep up with every wind of culture, doctrine, and the constant moving target offered us by our culture. Yes, a wonderful, adventurous journey this can be. . . becoming intimate with the Truth, Jesus, and our Heavenly Father.

Want to make better life decisions? Introduce yourself to the One who knows you best, God Almighty. His benevolence and love will always be the motivation to keep you on the right path and close to Him, and that may take some corrective action. Discipleship or to be disciplined in truth. There is only one truth. What a miraculous life we have!

> *"My dear child, don't shrug off God's discipline, but don't be crushed by it either. It's the child he loves that he disciplines; the child he embraces, he also corrects. God is educating you; that's why you must never drop out. He's treating you as dear children. This trouble you're in isn't punishment; it's training, the normal experience of children."*
> (Hebrews 12:5-7, MSG)

11

DRIVE AROUND THE DRIVE

For most boys of our culture, the passage into manhood comes with a set of keys. Driving! For me it was no different, especially being my dad was a mechanic and there were always cars around.

Two of my dad's younger cousins were race car and stock car enthusiasts. The two brothers were always involved with an automotive project, keeping the garage abuzz. I remember them as being the last of the "hot rod" guys as depicted in the film *American Graffiti*. They were always dropping in a new engine into an Old's 442 or changing out the transmission of a Pontiac GTO. Dad wasn't quite as enthusiastic to completely rebuild some classic automobile, but he enjoyed working on cars, had his own garage for a bit, and was always helping out a neighbor or family member repairing their cars. For him, it was more of a job than a hobby.

Cousin John actually worked on the crew of the Blue Flame, a rocket-powered land speed racing vehicle, for a time. Very cool. In fact, I thought my dad's two cousins, Teddy and John, were the coolest guys on the planet. I often imagined myself driving a high-performance vehicle in my younger years. I am blessed and fortunate that I have been able to check this off my bucket list—not that it is all that important as life matters go—but it is fun, and fast.

One thing I am so appreciative of is that the principal men in my life were good men, real men—the "greatest generation" type of men. They all spoke into my life on important things, character building things like honesty, integrity, work ethic, being generous, honoring women and elders, and taking responsibility. This is one of those "taking responsibility" stories.

I was thirteen years of age, the eldest of the grandchildren on my mother's side. The first teenager. I referred to my grandfather as Pop. I was his favorite grandkid, maybe because I was his first. Maybe he just made me feel like I was his favorite. Anyway, isn't that the important thing? . . . how he made me feel and what he made me believe about myself. I was special. I could accomplish whatever I wanted if I was willing to work at it. I was accepted and wanted just as I was.

Pop would often tell me that, as the eldest, I had great responsibility to look after the others, especially my brother and sister. I somehow knew instinctively that I could depend on him for anything. And, I aspired to be someone he could depend on, even as a kid.

Pop's hobby was raising pigeons. He used the attic of the free-standing garage as a pigeon coop to house the birds. It was my job to assist in the caring of the birds whenever I stayed at Pop and Nana's place. I would have to climb the rickety stairs at the rear of the garage with a pail of water to assure they had fresh water each day. By the time I reached the top step, there was barely enough to supply fresh water, as I inevitably spilled a small quantity with each step. Their feed was in a metal garbage can at the top of the stairs. "Always replace the cover," Pop would remind me, "or the mice will have a field day." I recall Pop having about thirty birds, some fancier than others, but a nice variety. I never realized how many varieties there are. I always thought a pigeon was just a pigeon. Just like other species of animals there are variations, just like breeds of dogs. Who knew?

One day, Pop bought a used VW camper van. You know the type. He was going to park it alongside the garage. I wasn't sure if he planned to utilize this VW as an additional coop or if it would replace the one above the garage. All I knew was that I wanted to try to drive this funny-looking thing.

Pop's house was on a corner lot, a double lot actually, with a huge side lawn. Abutting the back of the property were the railroad tracks of the Long Island Railroad, thus the side street was a "dead end," offering a small private road. The driveway went alongside the left side of the house into the backyard towards the garage at the rear of the property, then turned right, exiting to the side street. It was the perfect place to take my first driving lesson—at least, that was what I saw.

"So, Pop! How about showing me how to drive?" I requested in my best favorite grandson voice. "We can use the VW in the driveway!" My cousin Chip was visiting, as well, as it was some kind of a family gathering. Chip was the second-eldest grandson, a year younger than I, so I was often the lead on our ventures. This also usually meant I was the one who got in trouble. (Hey, no guts, no glory, right?)

To our surprise, Pop said, "Sure, just stay on the property," and he tossed us the keys.

"You're not coming with us?" we questioned, as did all the adults in the room. The women, my mom and Aunt Anita, objected most vehemently. Pop stood his ground.

"They're boys; let them grow up a bit." He showed us how to put the van in forward gear and reverse. (Thank the good Lord it was an automatic.) He continued his instruction, "Now, boys, you must go very slowly . . . keep the vehicle on the driveway, not on the grass . . . and stay on the property. You can use the side road to turn around, but get right back on the driveway. Got it?"

We responded in unison, "Yes, sir!"

Wow, here we are. I'm in the driver's seat and Chip is in the passenger's. We were just staring at each other in amazement, not sure if we were dreaming or was this real. "Start her up!" Chip encouraged in a hurried voice, as if the moment would pass and we would miss our chance. I turned the key and the VW engine started. I put our new-found mode of transportation in drive and, very lightly, I pressed the gas pedal, allowing the vehicle to begin a slow roll forward. We looked at each other, simultaneously releasing an excited squeal like two school girls just asked to the prom.

I quickly looked ahead as the vehicle advanced forward at about two miles an hour. I made the turn towards the side street, amazingly staying on the bluestone driveway. We approached the end of the driveway, emptying onto the side street. I turned left toward the end of the dead-end street, stopped, put her in reverse, and backed straight back about twenty-five feet, then put her back in drive and turned left back onto the driveway as Pop had instructed. So far, so good.

We then proceeded back towards the main portion of the back yard. As we approached the end of the property, I could either stop, turn right towards the garage, or turn left down the drive along the side of the house. Looking at each other it was decided: we weren't going to stop.

So, I turned left, initiating our attempt to traverse down the driveway along the side of the house. I quickly realized, "Houston, we have a problem!" This portion of the driveway was very narrow, providing no way to turn around without proceeding into the active street. This, I was not prepared to do. Even though we had only traveled a few feet, I immediately recognized the danger if we continued, and decided to abruptly stop hitting the pedal. Unfortunately, what I thought was the brake turned out to be the gas pedal, and the vehicle jolted forward. I did not notice a pipe extending out from the house. It only protruded a few inches, but far enough that I hit it directly, causing a fairly good-sized dent before coming to a stop. From inside the house, everyone thought we would be crashing through the wall, as the pipe we hit was the vent pipe from the oil tank and furnace, shaking the entire house as if a bomb had exploded.

Once again, Chip and I glanced at each other, this time in unbelief and fear as we knew we were about to "catch it." Pop came out of the house. Looked at the front driver's side fender, he examined the pipe and the side of the house, and instructed me to put the vehicle in reverse, turn the wheel slightly, and "slowly" back up far enough that I could open the door. He had me exit the VW and he proceeded to place it back to its original parking place. The day of driving was over.

Pop didn't say much, just a quick comment, "Next time I will come with you." *That's it? We're not in trouble?* I quietly wondered to myself as I looked back at Chip. We both knew our drive was over for the day. Chip was disappointed as he never got a chance to drive. Frankly, I was relieved.

"Maybe next time, Cuz."

Afterthought:
Because He Has Set His Love upon Me

The story of David and Goliath comes to mind, as David naively accepts the challenge of fighting the audacious giant warrior. Stepping onto the battlefield, he had no place being there— neither did I that day, taking my seat behind the wheel. It was a place I had no place being. But yet, as we anticipate the story line, we feel God saying, "It will be okay. I am with you."

Life is a battleground we must all maneuver and navigate through, a cruel, hard, relentless place many times. A battle-ground for sure. The Good Book says the "enemy comes to steal, kill, and destroy" (John 10:10). Sounds like a battle to me! Jesus continued in this verse, ". . . but I have come to give life and give it more abundantly." That's good news, but seems like there is still a battle. Jesus also said, recorded in the Gospel of John, that "in the world you will have trouble, but take heart, I have overcome the world" (John 6:33, NIV).

Many of us desire life to be without hardship, adversity, difficulty, and suffering. When asked, we usually acknowl-edge that life is full of these challenges, but internally we hope and pray to avoid such in our lives and in the lives of those we love. Perhaps our expectation of a euphoric life is somewhat askew or, perhaps misaligned is a better assessment. I would offer that it is amiss to believe one can avoid the trouble this world has to offer, thus expecting a "Nirvana" style life. Rather, one should believe or have faith in the ability to surmount these tribulations, to expect and depend on the One who overcame the world.

I am not suggesting we expect, await, or anticipate misfortune, suffering, and strife—God forbid—but we should expect and anticipate God's help as He promised: "I will never leave you nor forsake you"(Hebrews 13:5). We are instructed to think on the good stuff (Philippians 4:8). We must be cognizant of the fact that, as we grow, our thoughts and beliefs are influenced by this "world" or our culture, placing us in peril, creating faulty strongholds of false truths. Romans 12:2 identifies this principle, and directs us to renew or change how we are to think: "Don't copy the behavior and customs of this world, but let God transform you into a new person by changing the way you think. Then you will learn to know God's will for you, which is good and pleasing and perfect" (NLT).

So, what is the correct way to think? At the risk of being overly simplistic, I would say it is to believe that God, the Creator of the universe and you, loves you and is always benevolent towards you. He claims you as His own and has provided everything necessary for you to flourish in this life. Consider all the times, as you believed and allowed God to assist you, that He poured out His love, grace, and mercy upon you, allowing you to overcome and defeat the trouble that looked to have you. Look back to those times and places when God was with you. Maybe God, even now, is encouraging you, all of us, to step out, to be courageous and face the next giant—not to tempt God, but to trust Him.

*"For He shall give His angels charge over you, to
keep you in all your ways. In their hands
they shall bear you up, lest you dash your foot
against a stone. You shall tread upon the lion
and the cobra, the young lion and the serpent you
shall trample underfoot. Because he has set his
love upon me I will set him on high,
because he has known My name."*
(Psalm 91:11-13)

12

THE MIGHTY HUNTERS

Hunting is another rite of passage for many boys. I never was really that interested in hunting myself, but I understand the concept, especially if a boy's father is a hunter. Many times a boy will emulate those he admires, especially his dad.

When a son is presented with his first rifle, the event may serve as a passage to manhood. Or, perhaps it is the first time a dad takes his son hunting. I guess the same could be said for fishing, although for me, it seems less impactful. Many anglers will vehemently disagree, and I fully respect that, but for myself, as neither a hunter nor a fisherman, shooting a rifle just seems to be more impactful. Maybe because, when fishing, you put your baited line in the water and a hungry fish takes a bite. The event is under water, somewhat out of sight until, wham, you've caught a fish. Almost an accidental event.

With hunting it is different, whether with a gun or bow. Tracking your prey or game animal, taking aim, locking your target in your sights, and pulling the trigger are very intentional. As I remember, in many cultures, the blood of a young man's first "kill" is very significant. In our culture, this seems almost barbaric to many, but for the "hunting" family, it holds some significance.

My Uncle Charlie was a big hunter with both the bow and the rifle. Typically, deer season opens first for bow hunters and then later for rifle hunters. My uncle took the sport seriously and generally got his prize with the bow. He often encouraged us to learn to shoot an arrow and even had a practice range setup at his home. My younger cousin, Chip, became quite proficient with the bow and practiced often. Me? Well let's just say the safest place to be was directly behind me. You could never predict where the arrow would land—usually on the ground somewhere.

One day, our grandfather decided it was time he, Chip, and I went hunting. I would rather have gone with my uncle, as he was the real hunter in the family, but spending time with Pop out in the wilderness sounded great to me. ("Wilderness" is a relative word for someone growing up on Long Island. It was just thirty miles from NYC.)

I never thought of Pop as a hunter as I never witnessed him hunting or heard any hunting stories from him like Uncle Charlie would recount. Anyway, it was all planned out that this one summer's day, Pop, Chip, and I were off on a hunting trip in the Catskill Mountains. Chip and I slept the night before at our grandparent's place in Mineola, New York, to allow us to arise before dawn and get an early start in the morning. Pop woke us up before sunrise. We had packed the night before, so we just threw on the clothes we'd laid out, tossed our stuff in the trunk of the car, and off we went. Chip brought his bow. I brought my BB gun air rifle. Oh, yeah, I should mention that we were only about ten years old, so our arsenals were quite limited. No secret closet full of weapons like in the movies.

We were both fast asleep in the rear seats of Pop's Plymouth before we hit the expressway; like I said, the sun wasn't up yet. When we re-awoke, we had already crossed the Tappan Zee Bridge and were driving on the New York Thruway. Another hour or so and we arrived at the motel establishment that offered both rooms in the main building or small cabins at the rear of the property. I thought we would just pitch a tent somewhere. Pop just wanted to grab a normal room, so it took a bit of convincing to persuade him to take one of the cabins instead.

"That's where real hunters would stay, isn't it, Pop?" Pop hesitantly agreed. We would relax by the pool for the balance of the morning and head out hunting after lunch. Seemed like a good plan to us, since we were famished.

After lunch, we headed to the trail, Chip with his bow and me with my air rifle. We thought it odd that Pop did not sport a rifle. We inquired about that and he produced his service revolver, saying, "This is all I'll need." He put the weapon on display for us, a small .22 handgun that he was licensed to carry as part of his employment as an armed security guard. I wondered if he could bag a deer or a bear with that little gun, but what did I know? He further explained that he could get closer to the deer with his pistol than a big rifle. Made sense to us, so we started hiking up the mountain trail.

Chip and I walked very deliberately, scanning left and right for deer, mountain lions, bear, moose, something... anything. After about thirty minutes of seeing absolutely nothing, we picked up the pace a bit as we were anxious to discover whatever game this well-traveled hiking path could deliver. Our distance on the trail grew between Pop and us—not that we cared all that much—as the trail was well marked. Several times we were so far ahead of Pop we were out of his vision.

Then it happened . . . *Bam!* Pop took a shot at something! We ran back down the trail, to find Pop looking off into the woods. "What was it, Pop?" one of us shouted out.

"I think I saw a brown bear."

"Really, where?" We both scanned the woods.

"Look," I cried out pointing. "Over there. Is that it?"

"I don't see anything," Chip replied.

Pop continued, "I think it ran off!"

Wow, that was close. Almost bagged a bear.

That reoccurred each time we advanced a little too far ahead of Pop. Each time, he would fire off a shot with his .22—one time a deer, the next a wild boar. I thought to myself, *Pop must be a really bad shot, as he missed every time and the animal just ran off into the forest.* We never told him that he was a bad shot as we thought it would hurt his feelings . . . but he was terrible!

At one point, Pop yelled to us to scramble on back, as it was time for a meal before returning to the cabin. We were always ready to eat, and to eat in the woods while we were hunting was really cool. Pop produced three cans of franks and beans, pulling them out of my backpack (I was the only one with a backpack). You know, those little hot dogs mixed with the beans. "Hey Pop, ya gonna build a fire?" Chip inquired.

"Nope; real men eat stuff cold."

"Yeah," I said to Chip, "real men eat stuff cold." So, we did! It was one of the best meals of my life! Sitting on the trail, in the woods, eating cold stuff with my Pop.

I never became much of a hunter. It is just not my thing. But, every so often, I eat cold stuff out of a can.

Afterthought: Masculine Manhood

Being a man. *Gabor.* The Hebrew word. Said to be the most masculine word in the Hebrew language.

In the Book of Job, God commands Job to "stand up like a man" (Job 38:3, ISV). The idea of this word is "to gird your loins and make ready for a battle or struggle." The literal meaning is to "act the man," act as a man as the Bible describes, that is. Whether young or old, we are called to be *men*, not just males.

But, what does that mean exactly? Our culture displays two very different images of what a man should be. On one extreme is the tough, fearless, tobacco-spitting, crotch-grabbing, stubborn, foul, *get-out-of-my-face* ruthless guy. The other extreme parades the sensitive, gentle, indecisive, insecure, *in-touch-with-my-feminine-side* guy. This is a colossal dilemma for most men, who are asking, "Who am I?" Many of us figure if we land somewhere in the middle, we're good.

Let's get it right. Man (mankind, I mean) is created in the image of God. In that, we find our identity, we find our purpose, and we find our mission in life. We are to be strong in stature and resolve, standing for what is right and true. We are to be courageous to overcome danger, stand guard over those placed in our charge, and overcome fear. We are to love sacrificially, putting others before ourselves, especially our wives and heirs. We are to be sound-minded, seeking and displaying wisdom, using good sense, intelligence, and insight. We are to be honorable, truthful, men of integrity. We are to be humble before God and man. We are to be peacemakers, offering forgiveness, patience, grace, and mercy. We are to be responsible, which is the mark of maturity, as well as accountable for our actions. We are to be generous with our time and money. We are to be reliable, consistent, and confident, yet not boastful or prideful. We are to stand in the authority provided to us without being oppressive, heavy-handed, or domineering. We are to walk in the Spirit, developing and utilizing the gifts providentially provided. We are to encourage and edify, not tear down with idle words and harsh talk. We are to praise, honor and glorify God with all of our being. God calls us to be men of steel and of velvet.

But, where do we learn to be these "men"? Where and how do I acquire and then absorb into my very being the attributes of the strength of steel and the grace of velvet? In Deuteronomy 11:19, (AMP) concerning God's commandments, we are instructed, "You shall teach them [diligently] to your children [impressing God's precepts on their minds and penetrating their hearts with His truths], speaking of them when you sit in your house and when you walk along the road and when you lie down and when you rise up."

Our lessons are handed down, man to boy, woman to girl, adult to child, elder to younger. God's precepts and promises, among the culture of the day, yet without compromising the commandments. Not an easy task, but who ever said it would be easy. God has prepared the way as stated in Ephesians 4:11, "And He Himself gave some *to be* apostles, some prophets, some evangelists, and some pastors and teachers, for the equipping of the saints for the work of ministry, for the edifying of the body of Christ," But guess what? He also gave mentors, coaches, role models, counsellors, advisors, tutors, guides, and gurus. All master craftsmen to the apprentice.

The military bootcamp instructor breaks a man down and then rebuilds him for the purpose of being a soldier. The bronco busting cowboy breaks the wild horse to make it usable. The farmer tills the soil to make it ready for sowing a good crop. Michelangelo chiseled away the unusable portions of stone to release the image within the rock creating a masterpiece. God uses those He sends to us, whether family, friend, or foe, to make us usable to Himself. Let us humble ourselves to the Lord and allow Him to create His masterpiece in each of us.

"And the angel of the Lord appeared to him,
and said to him, "The Lord is with you,
you mighty man of valor!"
(Judges 6:12)

13

WHAT'S THAT TAPPING?

Have you ever come across a child who was continuously tapping on something? Beating on the seatback in the car or on a table? Continually drumming a pitter-patter? That kid who just can't sit still? Well, that was me. I can still hear the pleas of my father, "Dennis, can you *please* sit still and stop that tapping?" Even as an adult, I am the guy who would annoy you with a constant, droning racket—a hand percussionist extraordinaire.

The solitary factor that brought great anticipation and excitement to me in elementary school occurred as I was entering the fourth grade. You see, promotion to the fourth grade presented the opportunity to play a musical instrument, or at least commence the learning process. To be eligible for formal music lessons. And, as you can probably surmise, my desire was to learn to play… you guessed it… the drums.

On that very first day of fourth grade, I located the music department to register to be a drum student. The teacher in charge greeted me cheerfully. "How can I help you, young m— . . . ?"

"I want to play the drums," I interrupted, not allowing him to finish his sentence.

He continued, "The drum teacher is not in today, but I am sure we can find something suitable for you."

Now, I am not sure how it happened, but somehow when I returned home to be greeted by my mom, who expected me to be carrying a pair of drumsticks, she was genuinely surprised to see me hauling a . . . *cello* along with my books! Backpacks were not yet in vogue as they are today. Back then, we had that large rubber band thing with the hook to bind all the books together. I often found that the books would slip out all over the place. My dad resolved that problem by having me employ two of these elastic bands to cross wrap around my pile of books. How pathetic was I.

"I thought you wanted to play the drums?" she inquired curiously. I just shrugged.

Well, after a week of lugging what was more like a base fiddle, due to my small stature (remember I was only in the fourth grade), I was done. "Giving this thing back today, Mom. Going to switch to the drums!"

That afternoon, I returned with a . . . *viola*. No drums, a viola. The percussion instructor, I was told, was out again. I began to think the drum teacher was imaginary, or that the string teacher was using this ploy to recruit kids for his string section. I validated my acceptance of the viola, being the percussion teacher was nowhere to be found, presuming I could learn something about music. So, I endured the viola for a couple of months, but my desire to play the drums did not wane.

Then it happened! My parents told me they would arrange "private" drum lessons for me and that I should return the viola. That was a big deal, as Mom and Dad didn't really have extra money to pay for drum lessons. I had to agree to a few more chores around the house, which I gladly accepted, but the money was still coming from my parents' pockets. It was yet another example of sacrificial love. I was overflowing with appreciation and joy. "You are the greatest parents ever!" I exclaimed.

I repaid them by being serious in my lessons. I practiced and, as I developed in my percussion abilities, expanded and engaged in musical opportunities and experiences. My practice at the beginning was a drum pad and a pair of drumsticks that were more like logs than sticks. The pad was a square piece of rubber glued to a small wood stand. I would practice my rudiments every day, sometimes using my pillow in the morning before I arose from bed. Utilizing the pillow was quiet and it had no "bounce," thus helping to strengthen my wrists. I also had a snare drum I would practice on. The elementary snare drum was more of a toy than a real drum, but it sufficed for the time.

Now, as the eldest of three siblings, I was given more and more responsibility to oversee my little brother and sister. This generally meant putting them first, making sure they were safe when in my care—generally being a "good big brother." This was what Mom and Dad taught us. Be respectful, mind your elders, don't speak unless spoken to, giving is better than receiving. The "Golden Rule" stuff.

My sister, Connie, was the second child in age between myself and Paul. She was very sensitive and Paul and I would often compete to see which one of us could make her cry first. It didn't take much, as I said, since she was "very" sensitive. Dad would scold me, "Dennis, you need to be nice to your sister. You need to protect her and watch out for her. Do not make her cry or I will make you cry!" *Yes, sir.*

One Christmas morning, at the appropriate and acceptable time, my family assembled around the Christmas tree decorated in our converted basement rec room. Dad had "finished" the basement, transforming it to living space that we used for ping pong, playing pool, family parties, and such. At Christmas time, it was where we assembled and decked the tree. Christmas mornings, as we all ran downstairs ahead of Mom and Dad, we would see the array of presents and gifts. Excitement and anticipation overwhelmed us as we each took what became our accustomed positions.

Normally, each person's gifts were somewhat sorted into piles, one for each of us, including Mom and Dad. Their pile was always the smallest compared to ours. (That was the way it should be, in my opinion at the time.) That year was different, however, and, as I recall, fear began to run through my veins. It was quite obvious that my "pile" was the smallest of everyone's, even Mom and Dad's.

Oh no! Was I on the naughty list? The alarming thought arose in my mind. *Am I now old enough that I only get an "adult-sized" pile?* My mind was searching for a reasonable answer for this injustice. My insides were screaming, but I tried to remain cool on the outside. After all, I was the older brother, the other man in the house, and it was better to give than to receive, right? *Who are they kidding?* my emotions responded. *This is my worst nightmare! Dennis, stay calm, cool and collected . . .* I demanded of myself.

Paul, being the youngest, would have the opportunity to open his presents first. This was another rule in my house. Open gifts from youngest to eldest. *Who made up these rules? Not me!* I said to myself. Present after present, Paul continued to unwrap. Now, Paul was slower than a snail when opening a gift. Okay, he was only four or five, but he should get this by now: rip and toss, rip and toss, next present. This is easy stuff.

Finally, it was my sister Connie's turn. She was much better, having several more years of experience, but she always seemed to have a few more presents to open than us boys. *Maybe it's a girl thing.* I waited as patiently as I possibly could, although most of this patience was fueled by the dread of finding out the reason behind the drastic decrease in the size of my "pile."

Okay, my turn. Just two small packages. I cannot remember what they were, which means they were probably socks and underwear. Some type of clothing. From a kid's point of view, the worst presents were clothes. Ever try playing with clothes? No fun at all. I was sure Mom and Dad would have some explanation as I completed the brief and pathetic task of unwrapping my diminished fortune, but . . . nothing. We just moved on to Mom, then to Dad, then it was over. To all but me this tragedy was unnoticed, an undetected breach between adult and issue, an injustice of conviction without trial nor charge. Everyone resumed their activities as a normal Christmas morning. It was time to collect the ripped wrappings and enjoy a little time of playing with our gifts. Connie had some girly doll thing. Paul had some stuff that looked like fun. I had socks. I decided to help Paul unbox and setup whatever it was he wanted to play with. I tried to be happy, but I really felt awful inside.

One of our other traditions was placing on the tree the Christmas cards we kids had made for Mom and Dad. They would open our terrible works of art as they unwrapped their gifts, making a fuss over how wonderful the card craft was. We were usually engrossed with our own gifts, so we never really paid any attention to them as they opened our little works of "Picasso" imagery. After playing for a while with Paul and his newly acquired stuff, Dad said innocently, "Dennis, did you see there was a card here for you?"

"A card for me?" That was unusual, I thought.

I opened the card and it was a clue that, if I solved, would apparently lead me to a prize. It was pretty simple, requiring only seconds to discover the answer to the riddle. The clue led me to a closet door. What I discovered as I opened the door was amazing. I mean, take-your-breath-away amazing!

As I opened the closet door, there before my eyes, was a beautiful, blue-sparkled set of drums. I couldn't believe it. I stood there, paralyzed with unbelief. A real set of drums. Bass drum, tom-tom, floor-tom, cymbals, seat, the whole nine yards. Wow! It was the most beautiful thing I had ever seen.

I had often wondered why my parents were so agreeable to arrange for private drum lessons that cost money when I was taking music lessons in school for free. Okay, the viola wasn't the instrument I really wanted, but lessons were free and I would learn something. I am also sure they needed to figure out how to pay for the drum set. And, not just that, but to be willing to put up with the noise. (By the way, it is noise until it becomes music. If you've ever heard a person just beginning to play a string instrument, you know what I mean. Let's just say we had a bunch of cats hanging around my house and we didn't own any cats of our own.)

They never said so, but perhaps getting relief from that screeching sound of the viola was the real motivation for procuring me drum lessons. Or maybe they saw something more. Probably they just wanted to provide the desire of his heart to their son, their child. Something good. Something amazing . . . rat-a-tat-tat!

Afterthought:
Special Treasures

God created us with a specific design, and made each of us spectacular, imparting special gifts in each of us. Music, art, sports, dance, logic, writing, compassion of others, teaching ability, singing—there are so many possibilities! Some of us are acknowledged for mastering the "gift." For some, these gifts remain hobbies. But, all are special and unique and bring glory to God.

Sometimes these gifts are hidden or developed later in life. Perhaps you wonder, *What gift do I have? What value am I to God, or anyone, for that matter?* Maybe you feel you missed your window of opportunity to realize your full potential within a talent or aptitude within a skill area. Possibly, like a valuable treasure, your gifting must be sought after, discovered, or revealed.

I hope you know and believe that you are a "special treasure" to God and those around you. Not because of a special talent or gifting you may possess, but because the gift, the treasure, is you. This is the truth regardless of what you have or have not done with your life. Do not accept the lie that you are nothing, worthless, or forgotten. You are a treasure, a special specimen of God's handiwork. Exodus 19:5 affirms this: "Now, therefore, if you will indeed obey My voice and keep My covenant, then you shall be a special treasure to Me above all people; for the earth is Mine." This promise was spoken over the nation of Israel, but those receiving Jesus are included as well, being "grafted into the vine" (see Romans 11:23-25). Jesus is the Vine, and if we are His followers, we are the branches.

Jesus told a story found in Matthew, chapter 13, starting in verse 44. It reads, "Again, the kingdom of heaven is like a treasure hidden in a field, which a man found and hid; and for joy over it he goes and sells all that he has and buys that field." This concept was so important that he immediately told the story again with a minor difference to make sure those in His hearing understood: "Again, the kingdom of heaven is like a merchant seeking beautiful pearls, who, when he had found one pearl of great price, went and sold all that he had and bought it."

You and I are this "special treasure" that God gave all of Himself to have, to cherish, to enjoy, to nurture, and to love. Notice in the first story he just doesn't buy the treasure itself, but the entire field in which the treasure was hidden. He didn't just pursue the good, valuable part, but the whole field, weeds, rocks, trash, and all.

That was me, before I became a follower of Jesus—a field full of garbage. The good in me was well-hidden and buried, just like the gift of my drums, hidden away from my view. But God, who knows how to give the really good gifts, begins to cleanse, unclutter, and clear away those things that conceal and camouflage our value, our true worth, and importance. We just need to be willing to put ourselves in His hands, to become more acquainted with Him as He is the master vine dresser. For, as I know Him,

I will trust Him, love Him, obey Him, and abide in Him. I am, we are, you are . . . His special treasure!

> *"If you then, being evil, know how to give good*
> *gifts to your children, how much more will your*
> *Father who is in heaven give good things*
> *to those who ask Him!"*
> (Matthew 7:11)

14

BAND PRACTICE
—MUSIC TO MY EARS

Through the years, I continued with formal lessons. When I was twelve, I became part of a duo with an older friend, Irwin, whom I met via Boy Scouts. He was sixteen and played accordion and guitar. We were hired to play at a few parties, at which I earned my first income as a musician. The early experience of playing with someone I found beneficial musically, but our fame was mostly built on our charming cuteness as we played "adult"-style music. I guess they were amazed that two young boys knew these songs, which I later learned were called "standards": Frank Sinatra, Dean Martin, cha-chas, waltzes, tangos, the whole bit.

In ninth grade, I was invited to join a hometown rock band. I was only thirteen and the other guys were all in high school. In my school district, the ninth grade was still part of middle school, so this was a big deal for me, as I got to hang out with real high school kids. I also noticed that the girls in high school looked much different than those in middle school. As I was becoming more interested in the opposite sex, I looked upon this as an important benefit – more important with each maturing day.

Being part of this band was pretty cool and the players weren't bad, not that I had extensive exposure to other musicians for comparison, but the songs we performed didn't sound half bad. Our repertoire was only about ten songs, with selections from Otis Redding, the Young Rascals, "Knock on Wood" by Eddie Floyd, "96 Tears," Mitch Ryder's "Devil with the Blue Dress," and a few more. Band practice was in someone's garage (really, we were one of those "garage bands"), and as we played and improved, the number of kids hanging around—girls, mainly—grew.

The name of our band was "The Who's Who." I mentioned to the rest of them that there were two other groups with similar names, "The Who" and "The Guess Who"— both famous, popular, and really successful. The other band members didn't believe this was a problem and actually thought we could take advantage of having a similar name. We did not perform any songs from either group, but what did I know?

Then our big break! We were hired to perform at our high school dance, for about three hours of music. I saw this as a potential issue as most songs in the sixties averaged three, maybe four minutes in length by AM radio time. There were no twenty-minute songs with long guitar solos like in the seventies. We only had ten songs, about thirty minutes of music. Add in a little time between songs and we could stretch to, maybe, forty minutes, or one set. We were expected to play three sets. Lenny, our lead singer, said, "No problem. We just play the songs again for the second set and then repeat them again for the third." This sounded problematic to me, but what else could we do? We only knew ten songs.

Our first set came off pretty well with no major problems. The kids were dancing and "hooting" it up after each song. So far, so good. We were really stoked as we took our first break.

The second set started off okay, but then began to unravel. It didn't take long for the other kids to realize they heard these selections before, and they let us know this was not acceptable. They began shouting out other songs for us to play. We couldn't, so we didn't. Good decision. We struggled through the second set and wondered what we were going to do next. One of the guys said, "Dennis, why don't you do a fifteen-minute drum solo?" Still being a young drummer, my skills weren't that captivating to pull this off, and the question remained as to what to perform for the other twenty minutes.

Our lead guitarist, John, came up with the idea that if we claimed to have trouble with our equipment, like the PA system blew a fuse, then we would not be able to continue. "But, we are being paid to play!" I reminded them. Well, as it turned out, we really weren't being paid. Lenny had just told us that to get us to agree to perform. ("For heaven's sake, Lenny!") All we could do was to improvise and attempt to perform songs that were not ready to be performed. It was painful for all.

After a night like that, the reputation of Who's Who was shot. So, we changed the name to, you guessed it . . . "For Heaven's Sake." Ahh, Lenny, really?"

Afterthought:
God's Gift for the Soul

What a gift the Lord has given to mankind. Music. Sounds and rhythms and melodies and harmonies. Music that calms our souls, raises our battle cries, stirs the emotion of romance, sings of our pains and sorrows. Songs of bondage and freedom. Psalms to God, sonnets to honor others, serenades for our lovers, symphonies to fill our senses. Thank you, Lord, for such a gift.

Many people believe that music belongs to God. I am not so sure that is all it is for. Yes, He is the creator, the provider, the Master Conductor, and I believe He would say that, like the rest of His creation, "It is very good" (Genesis 1:31). But, I believe the greatest benefactor of music may be us, you and me—all people.

One example of this is illustrated in 1 Samuel 16:23: "And so it was, whenever the spirit from God was upon Saul, that David would take a harp and play it with his hand. Then Saul would become refreshed and well, and the distressing spirit would depart from him." I think about sitting in a doctor's office where music is playing to "calm" and distract me. Or the times when our favorite sports team hears the crowds chant as a stadium anthem, "We will, we will, rock you!" Even the quiet moments of listening to a bird's simple tweets and other sounds of nature affects my soul and brings joy.

History includes the sounds of the bugle blaring the cavalry charge, the soulful sounds from a chain gang, and the cadence of song as troops march. These all have a purpose, an objective, and intent. Just think about the emotional impact we feel when a national anthem is heard or the tears that flow when hearing "our song," causing the reminder of loss of a loved one or the reminiscing of special moments in one's life.

Whether blessed with a talent to make music or simply the appreciation to enjoy the sounds composed, the gift of music is a wonderful, delightful, and powerful gift endowed to mankind by God Himself. Praises, therefore, do belong to God for He is good and wants good things for His creation, His children.

I encourage you to relate to God through music. Turn your voice towards heaven and sing a song to God. Express yourself to Him no matter joy or sadness, in victory or desperation but "Through It All", as penned by gospel music artist Andre Crouch. Use music to give him honor and praise; not only is it an appropriate and proper use to offer a blessing to God, but it will bring a blessing back to you, as well!

> *"Oh come, let us sing to the Lord!*
> *Let us shout joyfully to the Rock of our salvation."*
> (Psalm 95:1)

15

MY CLAIM TO FAME

We all look to be recognized, to have our ego stroked from time to time. Even the shyest of us wants some accolades once in a while. We welcome, even require, to be appreciated for a talent or a job well done. We covet that fifteen minutes of fame—at least a moment in our lives where we can say, "I came *that* close."

By the spring of 1968, the original rock band I was recruited for in high school disbanded. I then decided to assemble my own band consisting of drums, guitar, organ, bass, and sax. I convinced Jody, a girl I knew from high school, to sing lead. We played music from The Doors, The Rolling Stones, Cream, Jimi Hendrix, and Janis Joplin, among others. Band practice was now held at my house, as we had that great basement Dad had "finished," We were permitted to leave the instruments and equipment setup. This allowed us to rehearse without wasting time breaking down and setting up each time. We were serious and rehearsed often.

Our claim to fame occurred in late 1969 at a high school concert when we opened for the great Billy Joel. He wasn't popular or famous as of yet, as he was still young and performing with the group "The Hassels." He was a few years older than I, about nineteen at the time. Even though they were a local Long Island band, I did not know them nor him. (As I said, he was a bit older.) The Hassels had some limited success, releasing two albums of original songs, which was very cool, placing them at a level above most of the other local bands such as the Good Rats, Twisted Sister, and the Rhythm Jesters.

During this event, our interaction was very limited, non-existent to be honest. They were the "stars" and acted as such. We were, well, the opening act—clearly not as polished or talented, nor as "famous" as they. I would have thought they would embrace co-musicians, even though we were younger, but they kept to themselves in the appointed "green room," which was, in reality, their van in the parking lot. I guess they saw us as just kids . . . probably a fair assessment.

We performed four or five songs, all covers for other artists. We were allotted about thirty minutes for us to break down our equipment and they to set up theirs. The Hassels played for about an hour and were really good, although they obviously thought they were beyond playing a high school venue. I thought I was a better percussionist than the guy playing with Billy, but he did have a very cool setup where the bass drum, instead of facing out towards the audience, faced upward. Who knows, if Billy and I were more acquainted back then, maybe I would be the guy on the drums at Madison Square Garden, now that he is a fixture there! (Yes, "You may be right; I may be crazy. But I just might be the lunatic you're looking for." *Dream on, Denny boy.*)

This is all more impressive now, as Billy Joel has become a great performer, songwriter, and celebrity. At least it is extraordinary to me. I had the privilege to perform with many musicians over my life—not many with the success or genius of Billy Joel, but some talented musicians. Most of us were not talented enough, hardworking enough, or perhaps just not lucky enough to "make it." For me, it was just not my path.

It is interesting how some experiences may not seem that impactful as they are unfolding, only to be a "wow, pretty cool" moment in one's life as time goes by. Maybe we are the only one to appreciate and value that special moment in our life. No matter, it is still a special blessing.

Afterthought: Humility Draws the Gaze of God

I am not sure why many of us seek fame. It is truly very flighty and fickle as it more often than not fades quickly. I have also observed that seeking fame very often ends badly.

Remember what happened to the most beautiful of angels, Lucifer. He thought he was the greatest thing since sliced bread, greater than God, the creator of the universe, including the angels. It didn't and doesn't end well.

The Good Book says that we should not think more highly of ourselves than we ought. Gifts and talents and successes are granted to us by God. If so, and I believe they are, then why should I boast? Think of all the past TV actors or athletes who were once all the rage, and now we have a difficult time just remembering their names.

Here's a secret I have learned: humility is powerful. It aligns us to receive the best things in life, that "abundant life" Jesus refers to (John 10:10), from our Heavenly Father. In C. J. Mahaney's book, *Humility: True Greatness,* he writes, "Humility will draw the gaze of God." Think about that. As I live in genuine humility, keeping my "position" aligned properly under God, keeping Him first, I actually get His attention. I draw His gaze! What an image! The Bible says in James 4:6 that "God resists the proud, but gives grace to the humble." For me, I need as much grace as I can get . . . boatloads.

I believe there is more value, more benefit in being thankful and appreciative for the moments and encounters we are blessed to experience. Reading my own press clippings is egotistical, hindering my relationship with God who is the true author of me, and who bestows any and all gifts, abilities and talents. For us to make any claims of our own is simply a lie.

Thank God for the grace given you, the life given you, the identity given you. You are His, made by God . . . for God. You are a star, regardless of whether anyone else notices or not. What a magnificent life it is!

> *"The Lord is my strength and my shield;*
> *my heart trusted in Him, and I am helped.*
> *Therefore my heart greatly rejoices,*
> *and with my song I will praise Him."*
> (Psalm 28:7)

16

THE BRIGHT LIGHTS
OF BROADWAY

As I entered my college years, rock music continued to mature and different genres began to emerge: hard rock from Led Zeppelin, Funk from Earth, Wind, and Fire, Disco from the Bee Gees, and Southern Rock from the Allman Brothers, to name a few. In my opinion, some of the greatest music of our generation.

Throughout high school, I was consistently a member of a local rock band, eventually assembling my own. Usually as we graduated and shifted our sights on college, many of these groups disbanded as members went off to school. Fortunately, with the exception of Jody, our members remained intact. Teri replaced Jody and we continued our musical journey. We now called ourselves "The Shades of Blue," "The Shades" for short. We focused more on making money rather than our artistry, which meant playing at weddings, parties, and other social events. Then our direction took an interesting turn.

Our keyboard player's cousin was a professional dancer, and she was dating this guy, Vinny. Vinny was a wannabe actor/performer and he had the idea to build a variety show—a modern vaudeville act—with music, dancing, comedy skits, and such. My band was to provide the music, thus we now became members of this performing troupe. Teri had a spotlight performance; the four dancers had a solo number and backed up Vinny as he sang a couple of numbers. The skits included all of us and were positioned in between the musical numbers. I was in a Superman skit where I played a woman. Yes, I was in drag, but I sported a full, a very full, Fu Manchu style mustache which, we hoped, would add to the humor.

Where we would ever perform such as show was a mystery to me at the time, but Vinny kept saying, "Don't worry; I've got it worked out." Well, after about three months of rehearsing, Vinny announced the news we were all waiting to hear: "We have a venue to perform the show. Guys, we're gonna be on Broadway!" We looked at each other in amazement.

Well, the truth was, the theater was "off Broadway"… way, way off. No one seemed to care, though; we were just excited! I never thought I would experience anything like this, so I was thrilled. We all were.

Vinny had arranged for us to have access to the theater for two days. The first day was for prep and dress rehearsal, to arrange the dressing room (only one for us all to share . . . a story for another day), sound checks, lighting, vending areas, and such. There wouldn't be any elaborate stage sets or backdrops, just two backdrop style curtains, so that was simple. We would sell tickets and hopefully do well enough to keep the show open for several weeks. Vinny also arranged for several talent scouts and agents, as well as critics, to be in the audience for opening night. It was all pretty exciting stuff.

We were at the theater most of that first day attending to a variety of "set-up" activities. There were no roadies or stagehands. Our stage crew consisted of one lighting guy and one audio guy. Everything else was on us. We had to attend to everything. "Ah-ha", I joked, "that's why they call it a 'variety' show. There's a whole variety of stuff that needs to be done. Who's mopping the stage? ME? Got it."

Opening night . . . the crowd was adequate, almost full. (Partly because the theater was not very large, mostly because each of us had invited every family member and friend on the planet. Pretty much everyone we ever knew.)

It was almost show time. The band was ready. The dancers were ready. Flicker the lights so the audience knows the show is about to start. Everyone in their place. Ready? Lights, camera, action! (Okay, no camera, just start the music.)

Okay, we are on our way, I thought. *No turning back, now. Opening night . . . way off-Broadway.*

As we performed the prelude musical number, the curtain went up and the audience applauded. So far, so good. The band was not positioned in the orchestra pit as accustomed, but set up like a rock band, towards the back of the stage.

The first act was Vinny and the girls doing "Willkomen" from the show *Cabaret*. It was a good number that came off well. We followed up with a spotlight number for Teri singing "Cabaret" from the same show—a Liza Minnelli cover—and Teri's impersonation was excellent. The message Vinny wanted to portray—the pitch for the agents, so to speak—was that our variety show was like a cabaret. Something for everyone.

As it turned out, all the numbers were executed well and the skits were funny, but the idea of a variety show format seemed passé, outdated, old hat. You probably agree. There was not enough "WOW," pizzazz, pop, or amazement. Nothing to really astonish the crowd, more like a Wednesday afternoon Vegas act in the "small" room or lounge. Just a little dinner theater without dinner, unless you call a box of candy and some popcorn dinner. Critics and agents agreed.

By the way, it is true what they say: "Never read your own reviews." Ouch! Good thing Vinny only paid for the theater for two days, as the show closed after the first night. Opening Night and Closing Night all in one evening. A very special evening.

Afterthought:
For Whom Are You Performing?

"All the world is a stage." William Shakespeare said it well. The roles we get to "play" are so special, so significant. Son, father, husband, business guy, a man. Of course, our women have their own roles as wives, mothers, homemakers, and professionals. Some roles are filled by either gender, perhaps by choice, perhaps by necessity. God empowers each and all. Each role impacts a life or, perhaps several, even many lives. We all get to be role models for those we touch, especially our kids, either in a positive or negative way.

There was an expression, a phrase, actually—it was an event title—that when I heard it for the first time I knew it would be etched in my mind and heart. One of those epiphany moments. A concept that changed my life forever. You may have also heard or read this same phrase: "an audience of One."

To live for an audience of One.

This catchphrase caused me to think about me being a performance addict—someone who always looked for the approval of others, whether business colleagues, family members, team members, friends, or even myself. I was always looking for the nod, the pat on the back, always trying to be perfect. I was constantly in this comparison sparring match to see how I measured up, that "keeping up with the Joneses" syndrome.

Most of the time I found I was unsuccessful vying for the top spot or at least one of the "medal" spots on the platform of life, leaving me feeling disappointment, dissatisfaction, and frustration. I was never good enough. I never felt accepted, part of the elite, the A team. I always felt I was a loser, or at least second best. This was a lie.

The truth is that our authentic purpose in life is to please *God*. The audience of One. We are made by God, for God. . . period. Pleasing God is, in fact, our ultimate single purpose in life. He does not expect us to be perfect, only excellent. Excellent in our effort, in being full of grace and love for others. If I focus on pleasing God, then everything of importance is achieved. If I am speaking to an audience or performing some talent or even writing a book of short stories, the only one I need to delight is God. If God asked any one of us to speak, sing, write, or work only to help or please one person amid the crowd – the person God had prearranged a divine appointment with to provide for a need – and we are the instrument of that provision (even if for just that one person), did not success and excellence occur? I say it did!

We are to always stretch for excellence, always learn and improve, always work to give our best performance before each and every audience, each and every crowd, each and every person. But, our focus is to be on our true audience, our Heavenly Father. He delights in His children. He delights in you. You are enough. I am enough.

With that in mind, let's focus on being excellent as we perform for no one else but the audience of One.

"Quiet on the set . . . action!"

*"And every creature which is in heaven and
on the earth and under the earth and such as
are in the sea, and all that are in them, I heard
saying: "Blessing and honor and glory
and power Be to Him who sits on the throne,
And to the Lamb, forever and ever!"*
(Revelation 5:13)

17

TV ROCK SHOP

When I was a kid, my grandmother would take my cousins and me into NYC for a day of sightseeing. We would travel in from Long Island by train just after rush hour, as the train tickets were "off peak," and thus less expensive. We would visit one of the fantastic museums or Rockefeller Center, maybe Carnegie Hall. I enjoyed standing on the observation deck of the Empire State Building where you could see for miles. Literally miles! The elevator ride up its one-hundred-two floors seemed to take forever.

After some initial activity, we would have lunch, always at the same place, the Horn & Hardart Automat. What a place! There was a wall of small compartments with glass doors, allowing you to see the food from which to choose. A sandwich, a bowl of soup, a piece of pie, each for twenty-five to thirty-five cents, maybe seventy-five cents for the more expensive items. You put your coins in the slot, opened the door, and placed your item on your tray. What was really cool was that, as soon as you took your food item out of the compartment, someone on the other side of the wall would replace it with another. It was a very special, unique and fun place for me. The last location closed in 1991. If you never had the opportunity to eat there, you missed a real treat.

After lunch, we would go to the RCA building, or at least pass the building on the way to our next destination. I loved that place. If just passing, you could see yourself on TV in the window. We would simply wave or make some facial expression that had us laughing, making a spectacle of ourselves. If you went into the visitor's center, the set inside was much more elaborate, as they often had special activities where you would be on TV. Actually, you would just be displayed on the monitors, but all the same, for a kid, it was exciting. I often imagined that I would be on an actual TV show one day.

Then, one day it happened. It was around the summer of 1973. Long Island's UHF Channel 67 WSNL had a weekly program known as *Rock Shop*. It was a program that highlighted local musicians. The format was a solo or duet act to open, two songs from the main act, another solo/ duet number, and then the main act would finish the night.

My band, "Mama Hey," was becoming more popular as we played our version of Southern Rock with a brass section, a unique sound at the time, something like Blood, Sweat, & Tears performing the Allman Brothers. We would be the main act on this hour-long program and the first band ever that featured a horn section.

As we arrived at the station set, we were directed to the specific stage where we would perform and commenced setting up our equipment. It was a typical layout, with the drummer elevated in the back, the horn section to the side, also elevated, and the rest of the band on the main floor. After the equipment was assembled, we were requested to play a bit for a sound check. This is when all the "fun" began.

The sound engineers had never worked with a horn section before, and, even though each had their own mic, part of the sound echoed and bled to the microphones of the other horns. The engineers had a real hard time getting the balances correct, unlike the guitars and keyboards where the volumes are all controlled. The horns were a bit different.

They asked if the horns could play more softly. "Maybe they don't have to blow so hard." *What? Sure, that will work. The guys will just blow more easily.*

We were getting close to "Air Time" and this was a "live" show. We had to get this fixed, and in a hurry. After some discussion, we convinced them to use a different mic setup for the horns and the problem was resolved. This show was indeed a "shop," where we were all learning and getting experience. Some of the sound engineers were still in high school, but they figured it out and we were ready to go. "Quiet on the set!"

Now the excitement was really starting to mount for me. The sound check was good; the camera check and lighting were good. The time had arrived. I realized that one of the dreams of my youth was about to become a reality. I was going to perform on TV. (Okay, it was only a local UHS show, but there were cameras and lights and a TV studio set!)

"Two minutes!" the director called out. We were not the opening act, but we were in our places and ready. After the first act, there was a local commercial spot.

"When we come out of the commercial, the host will introduce you and you're on. Two numbers, then we break." All went according to plan. Sound was good. We played well. Good camera shots. Then into a commercial break, followed by the other act to perform their final number.

After the last break, we returned with our rendition of "Southbound." We were cooking. The song was long, so it was planned for only one number. It came off without a hitch. After the major portion of the number, as time was running out, the host came on with us, while we were still playing, to wrap up and thank the guests. As the credits scrolled on the screen, we continued playing, finally fading to black.

It was perfect in my eyes.

As with most bands, we never went much further as our lives continued to morph with marriages, career demands, and life in general. Our dream of being rock stars started to dwindle as new dreams crowded them out. This TV performance was the pinnacle of our success.

Our lead singer, Teri, went on to a disco-style group, playing "Rock the Boat," or whatever. I was never a disco guy. The horn guys got jobs teaching in one of the school systems, and "Mama Hey" was no more. About the same time, the TV station also went off the air, leaving me with a sense of fantasy and illusion – no evidence that this dream actually came true. There was no rerun to watch. Just the memory in my mind. I will say this: what fun we had. What great memories we made. And, what a time I had on TV.

P.S.: I often tried to see if any of the Rock Shop shows were taped. I guess they were, but they were never kept after the station was disassembled. Now, I can only be famous in my own mind.

"That's a wrap!"

Afterthought:
The Purpose of the Spotlight

In our culture today, many of us look for notoriety of some kind, to be "special," especially kids. And WE ARE special, especially to God. But it is humility that draws the gaze of God, not our press clippings. Understanding that our giftings, talents and abilities, intellect, knowledge, and victories are all provided to us by God is the posture we are to maintain. So, why boast, unless you are boasting about God? All that we get to participate in, all the interest we attract, all the fame we are granted, is to be gathered and then redirected back to God.

This sounds counterintuitive. It is. But it is the road to true success, God's kind of success.

That is exactly what John the Baptist did. He was a bit odd, living in the wilderness, munching on locusts and honey, clothed in the "Armani" of the day's camel-hair and leather-fashion creation. He was "one crying in the wilderness," preparing the way for the Christ—gathering people and preaching baptism, repentance, and the soon-to-come Savior. And, when Jesus came on the scene, he gathered all the attention his fame would muster and redirected it to Jesus: "Behold, the Lamb of God, who takes away the sins of the world." (John 1:29)

Building our own fame for our own gain is pure vanity. As proclaimed in Ecclesiastes 1:2, "Vanity of vanities, all is vanity." Some translations say, "Meaningless, meaningless, all is meaningless!" Yet, there is no greater achievement, no greater act of humility, but to redirect our recognition, celebrity, and reputation back to the One that grants benevolence to all of us.

If I think I am the all-in-all, then I am a fool. If I submit and surrender to my Creator, Lord, Savior, and God, I align myself with all that God has for me, so I can be courageous, confident, content, and consistent. I can be what I call "Christ Complete," to be closer and closer to the likeness of Christ!

> *"For I say, through the grace given to me,*
> *to everyone who is among you, not to think*
> *of himself more highly than he ought to think,*
> *but to think soberly, as God has dealt*
> *to each one a measure of faith."*
> (Romans 12:3)

18

FIRST DATE

I think we all have memories of the romances of our youth. Some may be simple infatuations, a school boy's first realizations of the opposite sex. A simple crush. The time when the cute girl in class goes from being someone to avoid like the plague to someone who stirs us inside. The feelings that we've never felt before.

I remember an episode of the *Little Rascals* where Spanky and Alfalfa have created the He-Man Woman Haters Club. They have sworn to each other never to "fall" for a girl. Not even talk to "them." Then, in walks Darla, who catches the eye of both young lads and all bets are off.

It was my experience that when one of the guys in our group became interested in a particular girl, we all became interested in her. It became a contest as to which one of us could win her affections. How soon we disbanded our pledge to avoid the female gender. I mean, you could get "cooties" or worse!

But then, right about the time we start to notice those first few strands of body hair, nature releases the most powerful of drugs, referred to as hormones, into the unexpecting child, thrusting him into manhood. It is a time most treacherous, most perilous, often taking captive our thoughts and will, causing us to act in the most unstable and illogical behaviors, a time called "ADOLESCENCE."

We were all too naïve, all too innocent, all too immature to fully comprehend what was happening to us from the inside—the involuntary response comparable to the transformation into a werewolf during a full moon, or that of Bruce Banner into The Hulk as rage saturates his emotional state. This is why, to most parents, the teens of their families seem to have lost their minds, are emotionally disturbed, or are monsters. (Easy, Mom and Dad; it's only adolescence and we will all survive.)

Falling in love is a wonderful gift from God. And, like anything else in life, falling in love properly must be learned. Things like how to treat a female, open doors, stand when she enters the room, and assist her getting into a car, chivalry stuff. How to show someone "I care for you," for, up to now, I only thought of myself. When it comes to romance, we must learn the skills of courtship . . . we call this dating.

For me, it was the summer between fourth and fifth grade. I guess I was only ten or eleven, rather young, even by today's standards. Her name was Ellen. Let me explain how this all came about.

My mother's sister was much younger than she. In fact, my Aunt Ann Marie is only seven years older than I. As her oldest nephew, Ann and I were, and still are, very close. I never referred to her as Aunt Ann, just Ann or Ann Marie, as she seemed more my sister than an aunt.

Aunts are old, aren't they? As a good aunt, she often baby sat and took me to various places. At times, I was more like a pet than a boy; remember, she was only seven when I was born. So, as I began attending school, she would tease me asking about "any cute girls" in class or, "Do you have a girlfriend?" I was usually embarrassed and threw something at her, but then one day I replied, "Well, there is this one girl from class . . . " (As I said, I was only about ten or eleven, and Ann was around seventeen. Now the conspiracy commenced ... as well as the education.)

Ann immediately suggested I ask Ellen out on a date.

"A date?" I asked. "What's a date?"

She informed me that, when a boy likes a girl, he asks her out on a date to get to know her better. *Okay, sounds reasonable,* I thought, as a multitude of questions rushed into my young mind. *Where is this "date" supposed to take place, I'm only ten? How do you ask someone out? What am I expected to do? Where would we go? How would we get there?*

Ann said she would assist me and instruct me as to everything I would need to know about dating. She was having way more fun than I, as I had no idea what this "dating" thing was all about. She had this impish grin on her face . . . and I was in terror.

Ann suggested that I summon one of my friends to join us—something called a "double date." I informed my friend Paul (insisted, actually) that I was going to ask Ellen out on a date and I needed him to come too.

"Sure, where are we going?" he responded agreeably.

"I am not sure yet, but you have to ask a girl out too."

He was stunned. "Why do I have to ask a girl? I don't want to ask a girl. Why can't it be just the three of us? Who am I gonna ask?" All of a sudden he wasn't so agreeable.

I had no answers.

Ann proposed that Ellen probably had a girlfriend who would join us.

"Okay, I'll find out, but how do I do all this?" I asked.

Ann replied, "Do you have her phone number?"

Why would I have her phone number? I don't have any-one's phone number! Okay, no number, initiate Plan B.

It was decided that I would ride my bicycle over to Ellen's house, bring Paul with me for moral support, and speak to her in person. It was also decided that we would go bowling. Everyone likes bowling. I liked bowling. Paul liked bowling. Ann said that she would drive us there and be our chaperone. Okay, the plan was all coming together. Now, I had to put it into action . . . D-Day.

As it was summer vacation, we were off every day. Paul and I proceeded with the plan and rode our bikes over to Ellen's one afternoon. If she wasn't home or outside, we would just ride by and head home. If she was there, we would stop and talk. I prayed that she wasn't home.

As Paul and I turned the corner, there she was on the sidewalk outside her house with a few other kids. We stopped and began to talk about nothing in particular; then I dropped the big question. "Would you like to go bowling with us?"

To my surprise, she said, "Sure!" but said she would need to ask her parents.

"Who else is going?" she asked.

"I don't know," I said. "Do you have a girlfriend that would want to go? Paul is going."

She immediately turned to her girlfriend, Patricia, "Hey, want to go bowling with us?"

"I'll ask my mom," she replied. Ellen would confirm with her folks and call me tomorrow. I gave her my phone number.

That evening I remembered that I needed to inform my mom as to the "plan." I filled her in what Aunt Ann had conveyed to me and helped me plan out concerning this "date." Mom cut me short halfway through my account of the plot, saying, "Let me talk to your aunt." Her stern tone implied, "What is my sister doing now?" as Ann often conspired some scheme that was not always the best of ideas.

After they spoke, Mom said that it was okay to go on this "date" with a few adjustments. My mom would drive us, picking up Ellen and Patricia, as my aunt, being only seventeen, didn't actually have her license, just a learner's permit, and, although it was nice for her to offer to drive, we didn't want her breaking the law . . . again. Paul was to meet us at my house (he was just around the corner) and Ann would, indeed, chaperone us.

We conducted this rendezvous on the next Saturday afternoon. That evening, Ellen did in fact phone me, informing me that she had permission, as did Patricia. Wow, everything was a "go." My first date would become a reality.

Saturday arrived and I do not recall being nervous or anxious. After all, it was just a day bowling, right? Mom did the driving as she had promised, dropping off the five of us, Chaperone Ann included. At the desk, we arranged for a lane and rented our bowling shoes, when Ann dropped the bomb. She whispered to me, "Dennis, you and Paul need to pay for the girls."

I looked at her in amazement. "What are you talking about? Why do we have to pay for them? They have their own money."

She explained, "This is a date. The guy pays for the girl on a date. You want to show them you appreciate them coming with you, and be the gentleman."

I thought, *This is just stupid. When I go bowling with my guy friends, we all pay for ourselves.*

That is when angst really set in, as I thought, *If I pay for Ellen, I won't have enough for a slice of pizza." This is nuts. No . . . this is a date.* For me, it was my first lesson in romance.

Ellen and her friend, Patricia, were nice enough to pay for the pizza and, for the most part, we had a nice time – minus all the emotional drama and drain on my finances. I took a lot of notes, but as an eleven-year-old, I decided no more dating for me . . . ever.

Oh yeah, next year we were in fifth grade and all the guys were in love with Jackie. Me too.

Afterthought: The Gift of Love

Before you can truly love someone you must "know" and "trust" them. This is what we call dating: socializing to learn about a person and see who they are and whether we could possibly "fit" together. In today's culture, this can mean many different things and take different forms. Add the technology aspect of dating and we have a whole new dimension. Add to that the gender issues, sexual preferences, views on intimacy, and even what marriage actually looks like, and, well let's just say I'm glad I grew up when I did. As Archie Bunker would say, "When girls were girls and men was men." (If you're not sure who Archie Bunker was, just Google it.)

Love is a powerful entity, not just an emotion or a feeling, more like a power. Both men and women have done many things, both good and bad, in the name of "love." But there is another kind of love, that surpasses human love. In the Book of Revelation, chapter 2, there is a reference to the Church of Ephesus. Amongst all the good attributes of that church, the scripture speaks of the one thing Jesus held against it: that they had "left their first love."

The ability to love, to care for and desire others and God, is one of the greatest gifts from God to humanity. I believe the ability to love as God loves, what I would consider the appropriate way to love as God intends, requires us to engage God first. He is our "First Love." God loves us unconditionally, and He expects us to pass this love on to others.

This God-kind of love forgives, redeems, lifts up, and edifies. It should be selfless, not selfish. Our culture instructs us to think in an opposite paradigm, of "me first": my happiness, fulfillment, and personal satisfaction. As long as I get what I want, what I need, I will love you . . . conditionally. If you are not aiding me in attaining and gratifying my desires and needs, who knows? My choice to love you may be hindered and obstructed.

Jesus' exhortation to the Church of Ephesus in Revelation 2 was to "consider from where they had fallen," as they turned away from their "first love." Reading this passage has caused me to appreciate "from where I (Dennis) had fallen." It provides me with the reality of my initial condition, my depravity. Only through the redemptive sacrifice, the absolute display of unconditional love by Christ, are we restored and provided the ability to think of others first, to love God with our whole heart, and to declare, "I am second."

C.S. Lewis said, "Humility is not thinking less of yourself; it's thinking of yourself less." Jesus stated, when asked, "What is the greatest of the commandments?": "You shall love the Lord your God with all your heart, with all your soul, and with all your mind. This is *the* first and greatest commandment. And *the* second *is* like it: You shall love your neighbor as yourself" (see Matthew 22:34-40, NIV).

I would submit that this is the proper way to love. If we keep the cosmic alignment correct where God is first in our focus, attitude, conduct, and life, than we will practice and obey the commandment established, permitting the power of His love to affect the heart of those we touch. Loving God with all my heart, soul, and mind—and my neighbor as myself.

"So God so loved the world that He gave His only begotten Son, that whoever believes in Him should not perish, but have everlasting life."
(John 3:16)

19

FIRST LOVE

I think we all remember the first time we fell in love: not just an infatuation with or a crush on someone, but that time we really, truly, head-over-heels, fell in love. Maybe it was that "love at first sight" moment, or perhaps it was more of a "slow burn" relationship that grew a little at a time and then, one day, you woke up and *Bam!* You realized she was the one. Either way, it was and should continue to be a very special moment. This is such a love story.

When I first met Gail, we were both kids. I was fifteen and she was fourteen. It was the summer of 1968, the time between freshman and sophomore high school years. Gail attended an all-girls Catholic school and I was headed back to public school. We both lived in the same town, but we had never met before, later learning that our paths did in fact cross.

My group of friends was made up of mostly jocks or young musicians. With the development of a newly formed rock band, we devoted much of our time to rehearsing, usually at my house or in someone's garage, or I was listening to one of the other local bands. There was always a bunch of teens hanging out, listening. My introduction to Gail was via one of my drummer buddies, Gary. They knew each other from elementary school and were neighbors, living with adjacent backyards.

Gail caught my eye from the very beginning, but it took a little time to convince her to "go out with me." I believe she was actually more interested in one of the other guys, but I was determined to win her over. And I did!

Looking back, I've realized this is an important aspect of manhood, for I believe a man has the innate desire to "win his lady," not just as the "hunter" within, but to be the "knight in shining armor" in our love's life. To prove, and continue to demonstrate, how truly valuable she is to us. How she completes, fulfills, and complements us. I further believe a woman looks for and expects that attribute in a man as well. (I know, I'm a hopeless romantic, but isn't that what life's about . . . passion, the thrill, an endless love?

God loves each of us with such a passion. What am I saying? His passion for us is immeasurable and, if we are created in His image and likeness, then we are to have a great passion, too. Maybe that is the precise moment when "love" for that special person is birthed in one's heart. *BAM!*

Gail and I dated and grew as a couple enjoying all those special moments... the senior prom, graduation, summer jobs, college. In September 1971, directly after graduating high school, I enlisted in the Air National Guard, as the Vietnam War and related draft was active and I wanted to avoid being deployed overseas. My active duty stint was only a year, and then I was redeployed as one of the "weekend warriors." The experience was paramount in transforming me from a boy to a man. When I returned, Gail and I were engaged to be married.

It took a little time and much drama, but in March of 1976, we finally "tied the knot." It was a great love. A world-renowned love, at least in our world.

And, what a wonderful world we built together. The greatest moment was God's gift of our daughter, ChristyJeanne, named after Gail's mom and our recognition of our Lord, Jesus Christ's intervention in our lives. She is a miracle child (a story for another day) and the beginning of our "branch."

Yes, her name is somewhat of anomaly and not a typo, and thus the cause of numerous issues throughout her school days and beyond. If you were to examine most applications and forms you will discover most only have room for ten characters for the first name and another ten for one's last name. At thirteen characters, her name was often cut short and abbreviated or the logical cause for someone to assume that "Jeanne" was her middle name. For Gail, this was absolutely unacceptable, and she made sure ChristyJeanne's name was presented accurately on all formal documents. This became a personal crusade that spilled out to pretty much every form ever completed by our daughter. It would not surprise me if all current applications now provide for a minimum of fifteen characters, thanks to Gail's advocacy!

Christy married a wonderful man, Kevin, whom I refer to as my son, for he is an answer to many a prayer as we pleaded with God to prepare a "good man" for our daughter. Christy was a magnificent child, full of wonder and energy. Gail and I knew from very early on that she would require a very special man in her life once I was discharged from my childrearing and nurturing duties. I am sure God was challenged with this request but, as it is often declared, "God never fails." Kevin is all I could ever hope for and I am proud he is the husband to my daughter and the father of my grandchildren. Through Kevin and Christy, God granted Gail and me our first two granddaughters, Emily and Elizabeth, making our world a bit larger and more blessed.

In early 2004, Gail and I found our world being rocked like an earthquake with her diagnosis of breast cancer. Only a year later, in June of 2005, I lost my first love. We were married twenty-nine years. I was devastated. A friend of mine reminded me of a quote by Alfred Lord Tennyson. It says, "'Tis better to have loved and lost then never to have loved." Yes, I agree.

Gail and I had a great love. Many wonderful times and memorable moments. After some time to heal and recover from my loss, I felt life flowing back into my being. I arose to attempt to be comfortable and appreciative for some renewed perspective, a new vista of life's landscape for me. I approached each day with an openness to be as sensitive as possible to what God would require of me. And, although content with this adjusted life without my first love, God had yet a different plan for me. One with a new mission and a new love. And, as difficult it was to say goodbye, I realize how very blessed I am to have loved and to have been loved by a very special woman.

Yes, Mr. Tennyson, it IS far better.

Afterthought: Love Lost

Never to have loved? I have come to learn that so many people never have loved. Not really loved with abandon. Have never found the kind of love that our Heavenly Father wants for us, that which I was so greatly blessed to have experienced with Gail, by the grace of our Heavenly Father.

I believe the reason so many find it difficult to find love is due to their perception of love. Most want to be loved to satisfy a need, to fill the void God has inserted in their being that only love can fill, satisfy, and placate. The key that opens the door to receiving love is accomplished by our desire to love someone else. This is where we miss it.

We all have heard it said and desire to be loved "unconditionally," "sacrificially," and "selflessly," but yet we set demands, conditions, and requirements on others to "earn" our love. The perception is that love is an emotion that cares about self, and demands to have the chasm in our own hearts filled before it extends love out from itself. Like a balance sheet, to insure what we give never exceeds what we get, we often limit what we are willing to put forth of ourselves, based upon the inflow of love received.

Love is not about self. It never has been. Somewhere along the line it became "What about me?" Well, it's not about you! It is about *them*: about him, about her. Love is the most powerful entity there is. It's the reason the entire universe was created. The force supporting the continual existence of all things. The fuel that burns in the heart of God, that demanded a recipient of His love, resulting in the creation of mankind, of me and you.

Yes, love is demanding, most demanding. Love requires all of you, all from you, with no guarantee of it being reciprocated. It can complete you, filling the space in your heart reserved for this wonderful yet horrible emotion. It will add value to your existence and joy to your life. It can also break your heart when it fails to germinate, or worse, when it vanishes with a last breath.

The better we understand and acknowledge the depth of God's love for us, the greater the ability provided to us to extend love to someone else. God actually requires us to love in similar fashion, to mimic Him as He loves. To love with all your might—unselfishly, unconditionally, and redemptively.

I suggest you love as if it were the last day, the last hour. Love with a greatest of loves that spills out all over itself and on all those around you. Love recklessly, for it will penetrate the hardest of the places, melt the coldest of the cold, and give life to those that need to live.

I pray that you are loved, you have been loved, or that you will be loved as I have been. But please know this: you are loved so much more by a great and loving God and Father.

> *"Husbands, love your wives, just as Christ*
> *also loved the church and gave Himself for her,*
> *that He might sanctify and cleanse her*
> *with the washing of water by the word."*
> (Ephesians 5:25-26)

20

SECOND LOVE

Have you ever been absolutely surprised and overwhelmed by something you never expected in a million years? Something that wasn't on your radar? Something you weren't looking for, only to find yourself smack in the middle of a wonderful situation? This is such a story. A "second" love story.

It was in September of 2008 that I met my second love, Patricia.

Let's roll that calendar back a bit, about three years, and pick up with me attempting to navigate through a dark time in my life. My "first" love, Gail had recently passed after fighting breast cancer. She was only fifty-one. We were just entering the phase of our lives where we could enjoy the fruits of our labor, but our path would have a different ending.

The Men's Ministry leader of my church, Joe, had become a good friend and support for me as he was well aware of my situation. He discerned I needed a vehicle for coming back to the land of the living, suggesting I attend a men's Bible study right down the road from my office. Since Joe also would be in attendance, I accepted his invitation to "check it out."

Over the next several months, I began to "come back to life" and to my faith. As difficult a time as it was, I was soon to learn and appreciate this season of adjustment, as it became a very precious time in my life. In the genesis of this grieving season, I seriously questioned my faith. Not uncommon during times of hardship, illness, and the death of a spouse or a child, we often blame God or, minimally, wonder where He was during this time of need. This was no different for me, as I felt disappointed, confused, and abandoned by my God and Lord. Let's just say I stopped looking to God for answers.

At this same time, I was experiencing a peculiar sensation of sorts—an awareness, really, as I felt God pursuing me, saying, "I have not abandoned you. You are not forsaken. I will not let you go nor lose your faith. I am here and have been always with you, even through this most difficult situation. I will hold you, strengthen you, and heal you."

This Bible study was to be a big part of that recovery journey. Through this men's ministry, I became friends with its director, Scott. His wife, Debbie would occasionally ask me, "How are you doing? Are you open to meeting someone? I have a wonderful friend."

She quickly answered her own question, "No, not yet," as she looked intensely into my eyes as if reading a "readiness" gauge deep in my skull. Then . . . Scott's fiftieth birthday party.

It was a delightful celebration. Family and friends were invited to a wonderful catered event. In fifty years, a person develops many relationships, and Scott is a charismatic soul, full of fun, laughter, and benevolence, so it is easy to develop a likeness for him. I was honored to be included. As with the case of many a buffet-style event, the food line was a bit lengthy and growing. A group of five or six women were on the line behind me and, wanting to be a gentleman, I summoned them to advance ahead of me as I stood aside, yielding my place in line.

Debbie came over to ensure all was okay, introducing me to those in this group of ladies whom I hadn't met. Her real objective, however, was to introduce me to her friend, Patty, but she simply rattled off a litany of names as if announcing the botanical names for plants in a catalog. In other words, I remembered no one.

Shortly after this exchange (I believe I was plating some baked ziti), Debbie returned and inquired as to "what I thought of" her friend, Patty. *Patty?* I was confused, as I knew no such person.

"The woman I just introduced you to. The woman I've been telling you about!" she continued.

I responded, a bit puzzled, "Introduced her to me? . . . What about her? . . . Who?"

Obviously annoyed, Debbie retorted, "Patty! You just met her." With a wave of her hand, she referenced the group of women heading back to their seats. "The one in the red dress." (Well, to be honest, I did notice the "red dress.")

After an hour or two, still feeling uneasy with the idea of meeting "another woman," I convinced myself that a simple conversation to present myself would be fairly harmless. I mustarded up some courage and strolled over to the table where Patty was sitting, only to find that she had already left for the evening. "Well, you waited long enough," Debbie said dryly. She assured me that Patty was interested in speaking to me and promised she would get me her phone number. I thought this was a bit odd as, supposedly, Patty and Debbie had been friends for some twenty-plus years. *She didn't know her number? Not in her contact list?* Oh well, not that important. I told myself that I was not all that keen in beginning another relationship anyway, so, I put the event behind me. (By the way, it had now been a little over three years since Gail relocated to heaven.)

The Saturday following Scott's birthday bash, the men's ministry was conducting an event, and I volunteered to serve. Debbie was there, of course, and, when seeing me, reminded herself aloud that she had to get me Patty's number. Maureen (Patty's sister and a co-conspirator of Debbie's) was also there, and ended up being the one to provide it. Maureen casually jotted down Patty's phone number on a piece of paper, handed it to me, and simply said, "Call her."

To make a long story short, I made the call, had a great conversation with Patty (several actually), and asked if we could meet. It seemed like an "out-of-body" experience as I was listening to my own voice ask Patty out on a date. The first time in over thirty years! "Are you nuts, Dennis?" I wondered out loud. But, there I was, putting myself out there.

Anticipating Patty was just as uncomfortable as I was, I offered what I considered a "safe" place for both of us, suggesting we go to a music event being held at my church. Can't be any safer place than church! And, it was important to me that Patty understood my commitment to my faith. Happily, she seemed comfortable with that. We had a little dinner before the event and I began to wonder, *What is God doing?*

You see, at times I can be very cautious; maybe you're the same way? In these cases, I generally look for "signs." I try to follow my "peace," what I find peaceful to my soul. I look for signs of danger—"red" lights"—or signs to go forward—"green" lights. In this case, I needed big, bright, neon-style flashing signs, as my emotions were being stirred in a fashion I hadn't experienced in a long time.

Back to signs. First thing I noticed was that Patty's outward appearance is much like my first wife, Gail's. Similar look, body type, intelligence, good sense of humor, and love for God and family. But all this could be a natural attraction. After all, if I found Gail attractive, then why would I not be attracted to a woman with a similar appearance and character. I could almost hear God say to Himself, "We're going to have to take this up a notch. This guy isn't too bright." Sign number one.

Another thing was Gail, being a nurse, was always big on being properly hydrated, consistently handing me, and anyone else within her reach, a bottle of water. The joke between those who knew her that if you wanted to find Gail in heaven, you'd best "go to the River of Life. You'll find her handing out water." Now, on this first date with Patty, as she was getting into my car her initial words were, "I thought you might want some water," as she handed me a bottle. I tried to not go into shock right there as I took the bottle from her hand. Coincidence?

As Patty and I had dinner, over more conversation she asked me when my birthday was. I told her and followed up with a witty response, "And yours?" As she informed me it was June 7th, I almost choked on my rigatoni. You see, Gail's birthday was June 6th. She was just fifty-one when she passed. Patty then offered, "I'll be fifty-one." Get the smelling salts somebody! The story in the book of Joshua came to my mind immediately, where God held the sun in the middle of the sky, not letting it set for a full day. I felt God had stopped time for me for three and a half years, for that had been the time between saying goodbye to my first love and saying hello to my second. My mind was blown! Just as God utilized signs throughout history, here He was employing a few for me. I am sure He uses them for you, too. There were many more, all allowing me to trust Him.

I was and am so appreciative of the love Gail and I experienced—a truly great love story where I felt and knew I was loved every day we were together. I fear she may not be able to say the same of my love for her, but I understand love so much more now. I know that I was given a great gift in that first love, one that, unfortunately, not everyone experiences. I was afraid to see it diminish, to slip away. I couldn't comprehend how a man could love two different women at different times and not see one love diminish while the other love grew. I prayed and asked God about this—several times, in fact, as this was troubling to me. I think many times with divorce the couple "falls out of love" for one reason or another; thus, they *stop* loving until they find their next love. But this was different. I had promised to love Gail forever and just because she was now in heaven, that love didn't pass away, too. Now that she is gone, I am free to love another, but my love for her still remains.

But, loving another seemed foreign to me. It was then that I learned a bit more of the greatness of God as He expanded my capacity to love so each of them could receive all that I have, not just a shared portion. I'm not sure how He does that, but I consider this another miracle. In fact, I believe God is performing miracles all the time.

Patty and I desired to move this relationship forward, but we also wanted our families to understand and support us, as things seemed to be moving pretty fast. I needed this to be okay with Christy, my daughter. For Patty, it had to be okay with her daughter, Stephanie, who was only ten at the time. A month after our first date, I introduced Patty to my dad and my aunt at a restaurant. They fell in love with her immediately and gave me the "thumbs up".

Christy was a concern—not so much whether she would "approve" of Patty, but, whether she, being eight and a half months pregnant, could handle this emotionally. Christy had dealt with a great loss in the passing of her mother, and she had also lost two other important women in her life: her aunt and her grandmother, all within eighteen months. I thought it best to plan an evening for Patty to meet Kevin and Christy over dinner. This was a giant step for me, and I was relieved as they experienced a very comfortable connection making it apparent to all that God was moving His hand of blessing.

One of the big family holiday dishes was my mom's homemade manicotti. This was Christy's favorite, but with the passing of her grandmother, she'd decided she would never have manicotti again. It just could never be the same. We wanted our families to continue to become acquainted, so Patty decided to host a dinner the day after Thanksgiving at her home in Long Beach. The evening was wonderful as the obvious aroma of Italian cooking filled the house. Stephanie connected beautifully with the little ones, Emily and Elizabeth. We all took our seats at the table, said a blessing, and Patty's mom, Joan, began serving the first course . . . homemade manicotti.

Christy was taken aback, clearly emotional as we all thought she maybe going into labor! Catching her breath, Christy explained that the tray of homemade manicotti surprised her and must be an indication from God that He was very much in this new relationship. God can do anything. Oh yeah, another sign. Kayla was born two weeks later. And a few years after that arrived our fourth granddaughter, Jessica.

Patty and I were married later that spring, on May 16th. This was the only day available at the place we selected for our wedding reception. The "only day available" was also Patty's dad's birthday. He had passed a few years earlier, but it was as though he, too, was giving his approval. Signs, miracles, and wonders—some big, some small—all around us. (By the way, we selected "I'm Expecting Miracles" by T. Graham Brown as our wedding song.)

A second love, not lesser or greater than the first. A chance to do it better than I did the first time, but both equally as great. Equally as demanding. Equally as wonderful. Equally as fulfilling. The Good Book says, "It is not good than man should be alone . . ."

I couldn't agree more.

Afterthought:
Love Never Fails

Life comes with its share of blessings and challenges. Some challenges are extremely hard. Many horrific and heart breaking. "He causes his sun to rise on the evil and the good, and sends rain on the righteous and the unrighteous" (Matthew 5:45, NASB). But, in the end, God's blessings rule the day, especially if we maintain an eternal perspective.

God's ultimate goal is to be with His children for all eternity, not just while we are here on earth. Many of us have a hard time living this reality as we are so focused and consumed with the "dash." You know, the time between our date of birth and our date of death. DOB – DOD. The "dash"!

We ask the question at some point in our lives, perhaps in our senior years, "Did I live a good life?" What we really mean is, "Was it good *enough*?" But God's first requirement is found in our relationship with Him and His Son, Jesus Christ. God wants a relationship with us, you and me, that will endure for all eternity. Relationship, communion, abiding together, intimacy, and family are God's objective.

As we come into this world, we come in handicapped, as the seed of man has been corrupted by the sin of Adam. Established in us is a perverted interpretation of what life is: finite, fixed, limited by our five senses. We are instructed in Romans 12:2 not to conform to the patterns of the world, but to be transformed by the renewing of our mind, so we may prove to ourselves what the will of God is for us, that which is good and acceptable and perfect in His plan and purpose for us. Obviously, if we need to be transformed and think differently, that means we need to change from ways and thoughts that are wrong and not God's intention for us. Like I said, move from "handicapped" to perfect. From carnal to eternal.

As important as relationship with God is, He fully understands our need for relationships that are tangible to our carnality. We are created to love, to love both God and our fellow man. These relationships are life-giving to us. But relationships can also be hard — especially due to the fact that we are so often selfish. Give and take. I'll do this; you do that. The God-kind of love is different, very different. The God kind of love is selfless. That makes it really hard, but not impossible. The key is to learn how God loves and then do the same.

Marriage is a precious ritual and institution established by God, the mysterious joining of a man and a woman. Today, this traditional definition has been stretched to extremes. I am not going to rule on what mankind has determined acceptable, as ultimately this is God's call. I was blessed with the love of a great woman. I lost this love as many people have, and I grieved deeply. Then, God looked favorably upon me for a second time and brought me into a second great love. I am eternally grateful.

So, here's the question: can I love as God loves, or do I have my own variety, with its own rules? My experience leads me to believe that God is trustworthy with my heart, if I give it wholeheartedly to Him. He is love, and the giver of love. He is not selfish with that love, but will give it to us freely, even miraculously . . . time and time again.

"The Lord God said, it is not good for man to be alone. I will make a helper suitable for him."
(Genesis 2:18)

21

ENDING WELL

Unlike the other short stories in this collection where I shared memories, experiences, and things that inspired me, this episode has not yet occurred. Or, perhaps it would be more accurate to say this is what I am experiencing as I pen this segment. Where the other stories are offered in an attempt to stir the memories in you, the reader, to recall the special and precious events *you* have experienced, this is presented as my hope, my prayer, my aspiration for what is still ahead. Maybe you can agree.

I believe, at some point, we begin taking inventory of our lives—what we accomplished, what we didn't. What dreams and goals we realized. What is still on our bucket list. How we did in our relationships, vocation, life plans, and experiences. In some cases, regrets or things we would have done differently. *Did I do enough?* For some, it is about what we accumulated. For others, what we gave away. It's like taking a break in the middle of the ball game and having a stretch—a "seventh-inning stretch" (and thus the title for this book).

During the seventh-inning stretch, we look ahead to the end of the game, as well as look back at what has occurred up to this point. Reflect. We strategize anew. We hope the game ends well, in our favor. "Ending well" is a hope that, I believe, most of us think about as we mature. That's just a nice way of saying we are aging.

As of this writing, I have reached the youthful age of sixty-eight, and perhaps thinking of the "end game" is more in my thinking than it was when I was in my twenties or thirties. I guess it is fair to say I am in the "fourth quarter" of the life game. I am fortunate to have had a great example as I navigate this season, this mine field we call life, as I still have my dad at the fine age of ninety-five. To follow in his shoes is a privilege I have come to appreciate, honor, and respect.

I also know that I am blessed to, first, have this wonderful relationship with my father and, second, to still have him here on earth with me. I know so many men do not have, or perhaps never have had, a good relationship with their earthly father. And, even if they did, he may no longer be with them as they go through their "fourth quarter."

As a Christian, I believe we live an eternal life. We live our carnal life here on earth and then move on to our eternal home, hopefully with God, the ultimate Father. But yet, we hold on to flesh and blood until the last breath. I have heard it said that "everybody wants to go to heaven, but nobody wants to die."

For me, "ending well" means playing all sixty minutes. "Leaving it all on the field." "Not over 'til the fat lady sings." So many clichés. *Yeah, great, but what does that look like? Really?*

The Good Book says we long to hear, "Well done, good and faithful servant." I believe my dad will hear those words when his time comes. The main reason? He has learned to love. I hope we all learn these truths.

To love his wife, honoring her. Staying loyal and faithful to her. Providing for her. Praying for her. Being her covering and sharing all he has and is with her. Mom has moved on to her heavenly home now. She too, was a great example to me, showing me what a "good" woman is so I could find mine.

To love his children unconditionally, no matter what. To teach us what love is, not with words, but with his everyday actions. Once you are family, you are always family. God has blessed him with a great "branch," a legacy of children, grandchildren, and great-grandchildren—each one receiving his love, sometimes with the firmness of strength and sometimes with the gentleness of silk. As Psalm 127, verse 3 (NIV), tells us, "Children are a heritage from the Lord, offspring a reward from Him."

Sometimes families and siblings have difficulties with each other. My family is no different, but Dad's love for each of us was, and is, unwavering. To love his neighbors and friends. Again, with the act of kindness, a helping hand, a ride, the preparation of a meal, or some act of generosity. Always thinking of the other person first.

Jesus said, "They will know you are my disciples by how you love one another" (John 13:35). Dad wasn't one to talk religion. He just believed that loving people is a good way to live. So, how do I "end well"? With God's grace, no doubt. But I also know, for sure, I'll follow my role model, my teacher . . . my dad. Or, at least I'll try.

The same question goes to you. I encourage you to take time for a "seventh-inning stretch." Look back at your life, then look ahead. How will you "end well"?

Afterthought: It Isn't Over Till It's Over

I believe we are eternal beings, so our journey here on earth is just a part of what we experience until we "pass over the other side." The idea is to live well, all the way to the end of this earthly life, and to then end it well and live with God for all eternity. So, while we're here, we must keep living:

Keep learning and experiencing all you can.
Keep exploring both God's universe and your inner self.
Keep loving . . . there is never enough.
Keep forgiving all that do wrong by you.
Keep asking for forgiveness when you mess up.
Keep praying; there's never enough prayer, either.
Keep smiling; you look so much better when you smile.
Keep singing; you sound better than you think.

Keep laughing; don't take yourself so seriously.

Keep giving yourself away; you have so much to give.

Keep sharing the Lord Jesus. People still need to know of Him.

Keep watching, as the Lord will return one of these days.

I hope these little stories spur some memories and past experiences in your life, and inspire your own "seventh-inning stretch." I believe that God uses everything to show more of Himself and more of what He intends life to *really* be. We sometimes have some bad stuff to deal with. We are sometimes victims and have been hurt, deeply hurt, but God wants better for you. He doesn't want lack, loss, sickness, violence, or calamity. He wants you to experience love, His love.

Maybe this collection brought a smile to your face, a thought of a past time of blessing, or a hope to experience. I hope it made you think of someone who blessed you, and of someone who can experience a blessing *through you.*

"Ending well" . . . there's still time. Tell someone they are loved.

Love you!

Dennis

"His master replied, "Well done good and faithful servant! You have been faithful with a few things; I will put you in charge of many things. Come and share your master's happiness!"
(Matthew 25:21)

ABOUT THE AUTHOR

Dennis Labriola is a businessman and men's ministry coach. He has a passion to assist men in the realization of their God-given identity and to help with each man's journey to transform from a man of the world to a man of God, to become more "Christ Complete."

A graduate of the State University of New York (SUNY), Dennis initiated his IT profession in 1973, early in the "computer age." He established his IT company in 1980, focusing on Public Safety software applications, and grew his company to the number one market share position in New York State before retiring in 2017. Dennis and his wife, Patricia also assist those looking for entrepreneurial opportunities to establish e-commerce businesses offering guidance and business coaching. Dennis served on the board of LISTnet (The Long Island Software Technology Network) which represents nearly one thousand technology businesses. Additionally, Dennis is a former board member of the Applied Science Foundation for Homeland Security.

After a miraculous experience in 1978, Dennis committed his life to Jesus Christ, and in 2007, attained his certification from the Men's Discipleship Network to become a Biblical Coach for men.

Dennis resides on Long Island, New York, with his wife Patricia. They have two grown daughters and four granddaughters.

A free ebook edition
is available with the
purchase of this book.

To claim your free ebook edition:

1. Visit MorganJamesBOGO.com
2. Sign your name CLEARLY in the space
3. Complete the form and submit a photo of the entire copyright page
4. You or your friend can download the ebook to your preferred device

Morgan James BOGO™

A **FREE** ebook edition is available for you
or a friend with the purchase of this print book.

CLEARLY SIGN YOUR NAME ABOVE

Instructions to claim your free ebook edition:
1. Visit MorganJamesBOGO.com
2. Sign your name CLEARLY in the space above
3. Complete the form and submit a photo
   of this entire page
4. You or your friend can download the ebook
   to your preferred device

Print & Digital Together Forever.

Snap a photo

Free ebook

Read anywhere

CPSIA information can be obtained
at www.ICGtesting.com
Printed in the USA
JSHW061811191222
35156JS00001B/56